Give To Charity 20%
Let God Bless 80%

by Jon Liechty

Along with a desire to clearly tell the stories of my life I am aware of a need to protect the privacy of friends, neighbors, colleagues and acquaintances; therefore, I have used alternative names for some. –Jon Liechty

ISBN 978-1-63575-395-0 (paperback)
ISBN 978-1-63575-396-7 (digital)

Copyright © 2013, 2014, 2016 by Jon Liechty
First Edition

All rights reserved. No part of this publication may be reproduced, distributed, or transmitted in any form or by any means, including photocopying, recording, or other electronic or mechanical methods without the prior written permission of the publisher. For permission requests, solicit the publisher via the address below.
Christian Faith Publishing, Inc.
296 Chestnut Street
Meadville, PA 16335
www.christianfaithpublishing.com

DxDesign - Carol Dumonceaux - email: carol@dxdesign.biz

Scripture taken from the HOLY BIBLE, NEW INTERNATIONAL VERSION ®. Copyright © 1973, 1978, 1984 by International Bible Society. Used by permission of Zondervan. All rights reserved.

FORWARD

While many things can be learned from textbooks, sometimes the greatest lessons and principles for life and success come from the life of a person who has walked the journey of life for eight decades. These are the people I love to listen to as they share the stories of what brought them to where they are today. It gives a person a window into decision-making, family values, hard work, inter-personal relationships, finances, spiritual development, ministry, and career development. From these stories, we can learn to appreciate the blessings we have, expand our thinking, appreciate life, celebrate the success of others and laugh with each other.

In this book, my friend Jon Liechty shares the journey of his life. I have known Jon and his family for most of my life. His three children were closer to my age and so I knew them better than Jon. However, I know that the quality of persons that they were was an outgrowth of what they learned from their parents, Jon and Fern. Jon and I had more opportunities to interact because of work with North Central University. Over these years our friendship has grown and we have enjoyed fellowship in a number of settings.

However, I really felt I knew Jon after I read his book. It is an honest, straight-forward portrayal of his life that provides a number of insights into what has made him a success in God's eyes. If you read this carefully, you will find numerous principles that will bring joy and meaning to your life. You will learn about faithfulness and consistency. You will learn what it means to be a businessman who uses his resources and life to serve others. You will discover the value of networking. In addition to that, you will be challenged to recognize a point in life that influences every decision you make.

What I appreciate about Jon is that he has learned to be flexible and adapt to changes throughout life. He values the past but does not demand that things be done the same way. He probably learned this in farming. He is an entrepreneur who sees how things can be better. However, instead of complaining about it, he gets involved and effects change. There are many things in life that can cause a person to become bitter and critical of people and programs around them. Jon has chosen to enjoy life and adapt to changes around him. He is a person anyone would be blessed to have as a friend, and I am honored to call him my friend.

Dr. Paul A. Freitag
Vice President of Advancement
North Central University

PREFACE

This book may be one of the most important things you have ever done because it shows what God can do with a country boy who works hard, loves the Lord and puts God first. This book is a credit to the gospel, a tribute to your parents and it will be a blessing to your children and children's children as well as to all others who read it. This is a thrilling book; it ought to be widely distributed. It will be an inspiration to those who read it, and most importantly, it will bring glory to God.

Someone once said to me, commenting on my father's life and character, "He was a mark in the land."

The Liechty family has been a "mark in the land"—only eternity will reveal the extent of blessing God has poured through your lives, going back to your mother and father.

Daniel E. Johnson

LIST OF MIRACLES

Miracle 1 20
Miracle 2 27
Miracle 3 28
Miracle 4 34
Miracle 5 39
Miracle 6 40
Miracle 7 44
Miracle 8 48
Miracle 9 48
Miracle 10 49
Miracle 11 55
Miracle 12 56
Miracle 13 56
Miracle 14 61
Miracle 15 64
Miracle 16 65
Miracle 17 70
Miracle 18 84
Miracle 19 87
Miracle 20 90
Miracle 21 93
Miracle 22 103
Miracle 23 106
Miracle 24 108
Miracle 25 111
Miracle 26 111
Miracle 27 112

Miracle 28	113
Miracle 29	116
Miracle 30	117
Miracle 31	118
Miracle 32	119
Miracle 33	119
Miracle 34	129
Miracle 35	133
Miracle 36	133
Miracle 37	134
Miracle 38	135
Miracle 39	136
Miracle 40	138
Miracle 41	139
Miracle 42	140
Miracle 43	141

TABLE OF CONTENTS

In The Beginning 13

Early Teen Years 33

College Days And Army Life 43

Back To The Farm 52

Expanding Real Estate 67

Business & Travel 78

A New Paradigm Of Business 86

Friendships 90

God's Sovereign Protection 93

New Opportunities For Business And Ministries 105

New Leadership 117

God's Healing Touch 121

Additional Connections 124

Ever Greatful 142

Grandpa & Grandma
Witmer

Grandpa & Grandma
Liechty

12

/ ONE /
IN THE BEGINNING

My parents, John and Clara (Witmer) Liechty, moved to Brinsmade, North Dakota in 1914. Clara moved there with her parents, John and Mary Witmer, along with 35 other people as a group. The group included the Gerigs, Ringenbergs, Witmers, and Ehnerts. John Liechty, from his youth was adventurous, tired of small thinkers, came as a single man along with the group. They chartered a train to haul all their belongings, which included farm machinery, horses, cattle, and their house wares and all living possessions. Moving to North Dakota was a challenge, to say the least, stopping every day to feed and water the cattle and horses. The trip took two weeks. It was believed that Mr. Tom Ose, a realtor who owned a Brinsmade Bank and a Grain Elevator, had persuaded these families to come west to explore new territory.

John had a team of horses and a buggy to do his courtship with Clara, how far they would drive around town and country is anybody's guess. Brinsmade had a drugstore with a soda fountain. The town also had two restaurants, and at least three churches (eventually this Indiana group leaned toward the Christian and Missionary Alliance Church) available to young couple lovers. John commented a few times about the bad odor from the horses as he would haul his sweetheart (Mother) on a date.
John H. Liechty born April 6, 1890 to Peter and Anna Liechty near Ft. Wayne, Indiana, in an Amish home. Peter Liechty ancestry goes back to 1540 in Laudisvil, Switzerland.

John decided to go west and explore new country. Clara May Witmer was born July 20, 1894 near Ft. Wayne, Indiana, in a home where they attended a Church Of God of Anderson, Indiana. Although John and Clara grew up in the same community in Indiana they never met before coming to North Dakota. They were married December 3, 1914 at Minnewaukan, North Dakota.

Adam 19, Ezra 16, Jonathan 11, Paul 10, Silas 5, Reuben & Ruth 2

The only part of normalcy to any of this life Dad and Mom started with is the fact that children came along on a kind of normal routine. Adam was born June 25, 1918, Ezra was born March 8,

1921, It was time for Jonathan to be added on July 18, 1926, Clara called out and said "herrrrre comes Jonnie". The doctor came, with horse and buggy two hours late, and said you're here already. I said, yes Doc and I'm not going back either. Paul was added to the family November 27, 1927.

While horses have been the source of power for generations back, mechanized horsepower is just coming into being at the start of the 20th century. On September 9th, 1922 the Brinsmade Star wrote about the beauty of the steam engine. It is a combination of mechanical engineering and functional aesthetics. They were thrilled with the hushed sound of that steam engine when they got everything finely adjusted. It was almost silent, but a "moving" silence. With a hot fire, full steam pressure and drain petcocks closed, that engine idled with almost no sound. The balanced flywheel spun on one end of the crankshaft which rotated in journals well oiled with a recent twist of the grease cups. The intake and exhaust valves opened and closed willingly in this symphony of mechanical function. All that motion with the power of 20 horses, and yet you could hear crickets chirping in the distance.

My first memories of school, we talked German at home, were 4th and 5th grade. I must stop here and say that by this time in school, Dad and Mom had moved to a better farm only two miles from Brinsmade. The good part was it was a lot closer to town, the bad part that it was close enough (two miles to school) that we were able to walk to school every day, unless real bad weather came, then Adam or Dad would take us with the horses and wagon or sleigh. Sleigh trails in the winter were just like road trails. These snow trails would build up and pack hard and would be the last snow to melt in the spring. We could make home made ice cream from the snow and ice. The horses always knew the way home. I remember on cold days we would start the horses for home from school, we'd cover the wagon box with a big canvas and sit under there until the horses stopped at the barn about 40 minutes later. Sometimes the driver would bring along some lunch, or stop at a store and buy some candy, and we would have an under-the-canvas sleigh ride picnic. In the summer time we walked and tried to catch rides with the neighbor kids. Sometimes it worked but most times not. Walking wasn't bad on nice days. We could throw rocks at gophers or try to skip flat rocks on the water across sloughs. Sometimes we carried sling shots and fired at birds and of course we always carried lunch buckets, most likely karo syrup or jelly sandwiches with maybe a slice of dill pickle, no hot lunches at school.

Our school was a four-room school in Brinsmade, North Dakota. There were two rooms on the main floor, four grades in each room. Four years of high school and the principal's office were upstairs. The basement contained a large coal furnace and huge coal bin, usually full of big lump lignite coal from western North Dakota. The coal was shipped in by rail and hauled to school on bids, which was about 50¢ a ton to shovel off the boxcar and shovel again into the basement. It was a dirty, blackening job to say the least. Horse and wagon hauled the coal.

One of the things I remember about 4th to 6th grade was reading. If there was extra time at the end of the day, or before recess, the teacher would have me read stories to the entire classroom (only one teacher for four grades of school). I never considered myself a reader and still don't read a lot to this day, but my teacher must have thought I was okay. Recesses of course were everything from ball games to playground rides, maybe snow ball fights. In high school we played basket ball, but no foot ball. One ride I always enjoyed was called giant strides, which consisted of a high pole in the middle, with a wheel at the top, and chains hanging down that we could hang onto while we'd run in a circle and swing way out. The faster we ran the farther we flew. If we had a fresh snowfall, we played fox and goose.

I do remember fun times in school. When I was 12 years old I was able to get a driving permit, the reason being, to help on the farm after school. The day I went to get my permit I drove to Minneaukan, ten miles away, without a permit, all by myself. Dad told me to go see the County Judge for my permit. The Judge asked me, how did you get here? I said, "I drove". The judge just shook his head, but granted me a driving permit. My first drive on the way home was going past a field where one of my brothers was working. I thought I should wave as I went by and drove right into the ditch, I just turned the wheel and went right back up on the road. Dad would let me drive to school so we kids could get home sooner to help him on the farm. Having a car in school was a prestigious event in those days. Of course it allowed us to have a few boys and maybe girls too, to take up to town at noon for a 5¢ bottle of pop or some 1¢ chewing gum. I also remember malts were only 25 cents. On slippery days it just worked out to do a few wheelies with the car. The main center of town had a flagpole, and it seemed as though that 1938 Plymouth wouldn't turn around that pole without a good slide sideways. Then there were times when big brother Ezra would be driving the car and he would take us out on the lake on ice and there we could really wheel around. He would speed up to forty or fifty miles per hour and let the car go into a slide that went for a quarter of a mile. We had good reasons not to tell Dad. Although Dad had a few good stories to tell, like when they put somebody's buggy out on top of the barn, or loosen a wheel nut so the wheel would fall off or hide some ones horses, take the bridles off and let them hang loose.

In the 7th and 8th grades there were just four of us, two boys and two girls both years. I had a girl in the desk in front of me and one girl beside me. Believe it or not, they both liked me. My brothers thought the girls had poor eyesight. Remember, my mother said I was a pretty baby.

By this time I had to miss a lot of school to help on the farm so some of my classes were hard to keep up. When we would do workbooks, Margie in front of me would hold her book up as though reading it and I would copy some of the answers, Anna would pass me her papers. Was it right? No, but I felt it was all I could do because I had to stay home and work three months out of the nine months of school.

My ninth year in school was different from the norm. By now I was 15 years old. I really missed a lot of school. One of my subjects was English and most of it went pretty well except the book reports. When was I to read a book while working on the farm every evening? Yes, we would get home from school, and Mom would give us some cookies or a rolled up pancake with jelly and some milk to drink to hold us over till supper. We had 20 plus milk cows and we helped milk in the morning and evening before and after school. Sometimes after school I would drive horses in the field till dark pulling a harrow, disc or grain drill.

My English teacher really wanted me to pass my grades. While teaching, she had children at home and kept an in-house babysitter named Evelyn who was 14 years old had dropped out of school. My teacher would have me stop by her house occasionally. That's how I got to know Evelyn. We thought we were in love. My English teacher said Evelyn could read a book, tell me the story, and I could write a book report from that. It worked and I passed my 9th grade English. I remember getting an F on my report card, Dad went to the teacher and said Jonnie didn't deserve that F. The Teacher said, "No, he doesn't" but that is the lowest grade I had. This was in spring of 1941.

Now let me go back and talk about some earlier family and farm life events.

Dad was an entrepreneur in his day. In 1928 he had bought a second farm just south of the home place. The dirty thirties hit, the dust bowl of the times. High winds with dust in the air, hiding the sun, eroded the soil blowing tumble weeds and ground over fences completely covering fences and filling road ditches level full. The tumble weed, a prickly thistle, grew into a round ball shape plant, about eighteen to twenty two inches in diameter, then after it ripened it would let loose and roll in the wind. Due to hard depression times Dad lost the second farm.

On New Year's day, January 1, 1932, Dad got up at 6 o'clock in the morning and got Adam out of bed. Mom was going to have a baby. "Adam," Dad said, "You need to go get the doctor." None of us boys knew anything about a baby coming up to this time. Telephone lines were out of working order, some under snow drifts, the old style crank phone that hung on the wall didn't work, roads were blocked with snow, and the only thing left to do was go with a horse. Adam saddled up Beauty, our riding horse, and went to get the family doctor who lived in Brinsmade, two miles away. By the time the doctor got his horse hooked up to the sleigh and came two miles to the farm house, Silas was born. It was New Year's Day. Our closest neighbors, the Ringenbergs, living less than a mile away, came to visit. We boys of course didn't know where Silas came from. Our parents said Ringenbergs brought him and went back home again. Paul and I believed this for several years. We knew nothing about where babies came from by looking at what kind of clothing our mother wore. Mom never hung any of her under clothing on the out door clothesline with the rest of the family wash. There being only boys in the family, we had no idea as to what kind of clothing ladies wore. We boys didn't know that babies were breast-fed.

MIRACLE 1 As long as we're talking about Silas, I remember when Dad was backing the Model T Ford out of the garage. Silas, who was one year and nine months old at the time, was backed over with the back wheel of the Model T. Dad stopped, picked him up as he was out of breath, (I saw this with my own eyes) and carried him to the house. I think Dad and Mom's prayers brought him back, they never took him to a doctor. Of course, Silas was always tough and a survivor.

Our Dad was real curious about any kind of church activities he heard about, and one of his adventures was to take us to a camp meeting 250 miles from home. I was only seven years old (1933) when Dad hooked our 1926 Model T Ford to a 4-wheel flat top trailer. Mom loaded groceries and bedding for five days supply. What kind of groceries would you take without a refrigerator or a microwave? Dad loaded a tent for sleeping and covered it all with a big tarpaulin and ropes, and off we went to Lake Geneva camp meeting at Alexandria, Minnesota. Adam must have gotten up set, he got up in his sleep, crawled through a fence and went looking for horses. Dad took us fishing early in the mornings. Lake Geneva had a lot of little sunfish that Mom would fry up for lunch. Then Dad with his cap turned side ways and smile on his face would sing:

        Bread and fish upon the fire,
        Come and fill your heart's desire.

On February 17th, 1935 Reuben and Ruth joined the family. By this time I was old enough to know how they got here, but was still not sure about Silas. When the twins were born, Reuben appeared to be the weaker one of the two. Being born right at home, when we got up in the morning Reuben was in the oven of the kitchen range, a wood and coal burner that had a reservoir tank at one end that kept hot water. I saw that first hand. Mom had put him in there to warm him up. These were two six pound babies, they fit in the palm of our hand. The doctor came out to see mom later.

At that time they did not know Ruth was the weaker of the two. She had an open-heart valve that didn't work right. Her fingers and toes always looked blue. She was a very smart and cute little girl. Mother would sew little dresses, bonnets and clothing for her only girl. She put a lot of ribbons in Ruthie's hair. She was so very proud of her little girl. Mom's only daughter passed away at age 4 ½. This was a big disappointment to our mother. She always kept a positive attitude.

Earlier I mentioned the 1926 Model T Ford, but there was also a 1928 4-door Buick Sedan at the farm, it looked big and prestigious standing beside the model T. The whereabouts or where it came from I never knew. This Buick, big as it was, was very maneuverable with Dad at the wheel. It made many field trips, hauling lunch to farm helpers and threshers. It would pull large grain trailers of wheat from the field to the bin site. Wheat, oats and corn were all shoveled into the granary bins, by hand, using a scoop shovel. This was heavy, hard, sweaty work that put lots of muscle on farm boys. There were no grain augers in those days. Dad and the Buick could get the cows and horses home from the pastures and still take us to church on Sunday and mid-week

Model T Ford used to peddle Watkins products 1934-36

Bible study. Church and Bible study were never missed and there was never farm work on Sundays. One time our big herd bull ran off to Brinsmade and got into another herd of cows. Dad took the big Buick and separated the bull away from the cows by going back and forth and in circles. You cannot imagine the amount of dust and dirt that flew into the air as the tires were spinning and sliding on the grass.

The Model T Ford was used, as I remember, by Adam and Ezra to peddle Watkins Products from 1934 to 1936. They went from farm to farm, selling Watkins products, to help make a living for the family. Farmers were far from town and they would buy from them. Watkins vanilla, red lineament, and two different kinds of salve ointments for both man and beast were big sellers.

During these early winter years Dad, in a shop heated by wood and coal, began building a travel trailer. We never knew why he started some projects and what he was thinking but most times things ended up right. In the winter of 1936 he was ready to go.

The trailer had a stove and icebox and there was a place for all nine of us to sleep. Dad had made four spring-type beds, in an upper deck fashion, held up by two inch well pipes, for us four oldest boys to sleep on. This was above mom and dad's bed at one end of the camper. It was good we had an open ventilator in the ceiling above us four boys. Mom and dad's bed was a studio couch that we sat on in the daytime. We hooked up the 1934 Chevy Sedan, dad traded the 1926 model T Ford for this four door sedan, and away we went to Indiana to our Grandpa Liechty's farm. This was an Amish type farm. There was no electricity in the house, barn, or else where. They had kerosene lamps in the house and carried railroad type lanterns in the barn. We stayed there until after New Year's. He talked his brother, Uncle Silas, who had also built a travel trailer, into joining him and going to Florida. Uncle Silas's family was eight and we were nine for a party of 17. We were only a few miles from Grandpa's farm when Uncle Silas hit some ice and flipped over his camper, spreading eggs and the oats that he packed the eggs into, all over the inside of the camper. They set the camper back on its wheels and kept going, determined to go on. We over-nighted at gas stations, grocery store lots, parks or whatever looked good. There were no KOA with camper hook ups. Our dad and my uncle were ahead of their times. No one traveled all winter in a 7 X 24 ft. trailer in those days. We did have a 6-volt light system that ran off two car batteries. Our neighbors called us gypsies. We finally landed near Plant City, Florida, the strawberry capital of the world. Dad negotiated with two farmers to pick their strawberries into small one quart size boxes for three cents a quart. They let us park our homemade campers in their farmyards and have access to outdoor privies (toilets).

The picking was ½ day job each day. We worked one day at

Homemade camper Dad built, went to Florida in 1936 and to California in 1937

one farm and the next day at the other farm, alternating every other day. Some days were very warm. Omer, Uncle Silas' son, would lay on the ground to pick berries, some of the rest of us did too. The farmer would call out, "do you want a pillow?"

The afternoons were fun times for two sets of cousins playing softball, volleyball and swimming. Our dads gave us ½ cent per quart of berries we picked for our spending money. The dads got the other 2-½ cents to use for groceries.

We returned back to North Dakota the middle of March 1937. The boys of school age went back to school until the end of school year and everybody pitched in for another year of farming. Nineteen thirty-seven was probably the first good farm year since the depression of the thirties. I don't remember much about the depression. It seemed I grew up working as far back as I could remember, so when better times came it was work as usual, nothing changed. We always milked, 20 cows or more, by hand.

Nineteen thirty-seven being a good year at the farm, 20-bushel wheat yields at near $3.00 a bushel, Dad traded off the 1934 Chevrolet for a new 1937 Dodge 4-door Sedan. Now his roaming fever stirred inside him and away we went to California for the winter of 1937-1938. That winter we parked on a side street right by Angeles Temple. Amie Semple McPherson, founder and pastor, built this large auditorium. This was a large two-balcony church that had meetings every night. Each weekend featured a different illustrated Bible story plus other topics like Jack and The Beanstalk or The Cow Jumped Over The Moon.

The big round roof haymow provided a lot of fun for us boys. At certain seasons the hay was all gone and we could swing a length of 50 feet from one end to the other. At times we would tie Shep, our dog, in the ropes and let him swing. He barked and growled and really got mad at times because of the wild ride. Our Dad built this barn, as well as the house, garage, elevator and other buildings. Our Uncle, Adam Witmer, helped build the barn. Adam said Dad would cut a piece of board, on the ground, hand it up to

The two dogs we all played with.

Big barn we often played in also 41 Buick mentioned in book.

Adam and the piece fit every time. Dad was a very good builder and I can remember when Dad was hired to supervise the large auditorium at Lakewood Park Bible campgrounds.

Dad nursed a flock of tame pigeons in the haymow and once a year we would go up and harvest them. They had a big box at one end where they hatched their young. The box had both inside and outside entrants for the birds. It was fun to listen to their humming and cooing at night. Catching them as they flew around was a challenge and sometimes we got a splatter of poop on the nose or in the eye. When caught these birds were feather picked and dressed ready to cook for the kitchen table.

His eye is on the sparrow.

Look people in the eye.

Floss your teeth.

Have a dog					Life's little instructions

MIRACLE 2 Bad luck prevailed also as I slid head first down off the big hay pile, up in the barn, down through the hole where we put hay down for the horses, landed on my nose as I hit the edge of the manger that the horses were tied to. This was serious because my nose was bent 40 degrees to the right, I could have been killed. Dad rushed me to Dr. Vigland, the doctor who I'm sure delivered me at birth at the house. He took one look and pushed my nose right back straight. I remember he held up a yardstick as a straight edge to get my nose back in line straight enough.

One other event at the barn was jumping off the top of the barn onto a wagon load of hay 20 feet below. One time we threw the dog off the barn into the hay pile. Old Shep was a good sport and always followed us if he could climb the obstacles. Shep had the misfortune of getting one of his hind legs cut up in a mower. It was unbelievable how well he could keep up with us with one stiff leg. Shep would always keep other animals like rabbits, raccoons, weasels, foxes and skunks out of the yard. It was very evident when he tussled with a skunk. Shep was a friend to the whole family. Mother always fed him good food off the table.

Sunday was always a relaxing day because we didn't work on Sunday.

Remember the Sabbath day to keep it holy.
Be forgiving of yourself and others.
Commit yourself to constant improvement.
Make new friends but cherish the old ones.
Take responsibility for every area of your life.
Be there when people need you.
Treat everyone you meet like you want to be treated.
Life's Little Instructions

By this time Paul and I were 12 to 14 years old and still up to tricks! As we were looking for entertainment, one thing we enjoyed was driving the tractors. Paul and I always got stuck with driving the horses in the field while Adam and Ezra got to drive the two tractors because they were older, when actually the horses were a lot more dangerous to work with than the tractors.

Paul and I built a house on wheels, carried by an old wagon, that we took camping to a vacant farmstead a quarter mile away. Besides sleeping in there we had water, crackers, and candy. Our couch in the camper was the seat out of an old worn out car. Mom wouldn't let us cook because of fire danger.

During the ages of 12 to 18 we needed some spending money. We had to make our own. A lot of our money was made by hunting and trapping. We would trap fox, shoot Jack Rabbits and pull skunks out of culverts and from under old vacant houses. We retrieved as many as 17 skunks from under one old house. Working in the basement of the house the skunk squirt odor got so heavy we would need to go outside to cough, one time Ezra threw up it was so bad. Skunk hides were worth about two dollars each, so to us boys we were really in the money. Sometimes our hunts got pretty wild. I remember going with the Grasser boys to run after fox. They took their dad's truck and Paul and I were in the back leaning over the cab trying to shoot going 30 miles an hour over rough fields. On these chases we basically only got our guns emptied. Our shots went everywhere except on our target. The drivers didn't stop for gates, fences or rock piles. All they knew was to floorboard the throttle. I hope Mr. Grasser didn't think that Paul and I wrecked his truck.

MIRACLE 3 One time Paul and I were pulling skunks from a culvert, Paul at one end and I at the other. I got excited and shot at a skunk in the culvert and the bullet ricocheted through the culvert and landed in Paul's hand between his thumb and first finger. Dr. Vigland removed the bullet and sewed his hand back together. I cried for two days and thought how badly I would have felt if I had killed him.

Another way us boys collected our spending money, after harvest and threshing, Dad would let us take horses and a hay rake out in the wheat fields and we would rake the loose grain into piles. Then we would load the piles of grain into wagons and haul to the threshing machine. We got to keep the money from the wheat we sold.

Another way was to hunt crows and gophers. At the county fair they would pay a bounty for gopher tails and crows legs. As far back as Saturday, July 4th, 1914, the Brinsmade Star announced having GOPHER DAYS. That day Harvey Herman was announced winner of the contest bringing in over 2000 gopher tails. That's how the celebration began. The country side is over run with yellow gophers. They dig up young plants in the field, eat grain before it can be harvested, dig holes and burrows everywhere. A few years earlier, North Dakota began offering a bounty of a penny for every tail they could bring to the Court House. These animals were real pests to farmers in the recession of the dirty thirties. Gophers were everywhere, seemed to increase faster than any good crops would grow in the dust of the dry years. Crows were very hard on pheasant, partridge and prairie chicken nests. Crows would destroy the nests, eat the eggs, and the little birds if they were hatched. A 5-cent bounty was paid for each pair of crow legs.

Then too, we would walk road ditches looking for empty beer bottles. These bottles where worth five to twenty five cents each.

There were no litter laws, back in them days.

Gopher days at Brinsmade also included a horse pulling contest. I love to watch horses pull! There is probably nothing more beautiful than a well matched pair of draft horses at full draw force – percherons especially. All horses love to run, but draft horses love to pull. Necks arched, heads down, every muscle taut, both beasts pulling equally on the traces. With the driver whistling, yelling and slapping the reigns, they seem to pull for the sake of pulling, for the challenge.

Leave everything a little better than you found it.

Plant a tree on your birthday.

Plant flowers every spring.

                                      Life's Little Instructions

During this period of our age, Dad and Mom were really involved in supporting and working with the church ministry. It seemed as though we kept all the traveling evangelists and pastors at our house. Some stayed a few days while others stayed a few months. Some of them would sit on the couch all day waiting for The Spirit to move them. We had fun with most of them, but the preachers always tried to convert us boys. We were expected to be up at the altar every meeting. I'm sure it was good for us, but it got to be routine and we'd lose the impact.

Candice and Eliza attended our church. Dad and Mom took them under their wing and they spent a lot of time at our house. They had gained the name of "Old Ladies" by most all people. This was because of the long full skirt dresses they wore. We boys referred to them as paratroopers. We would most generally pick them up for church.

At this time we had a 1941 Buick with electric windows. Silas would pick up the ladies for church, and as they were riding along, he would pop open different windows up and down. The two ladies thought it was the Holy Ghost opening the windows. They really got the victory!

One Sunday after church we went to Frank and Francis Harris' place for dinner. Frank was a great sheep man and always had lots of them around. These people had a pretty daughter, Ruth. Paul always thought he was going with her. Then they would try to hook me up with La Verne Lass. It was a good idea, but nothing ever became of that deal. These were two young church girls that we thought needed dates.

This was in the 30s, the weather was dry and Frank showed us how the grasshoppers were eating up his yard fence. Grasshoppers were everywhere. They would fly in droves like clouds in the sky. Grasshoppers flourish best in dry hot weather.

That same day Adam was driving on the way home when a tire blew out and we rolled over an almost new 1937 Dodge. No one was hurt. We set the Dodge back up on all four and drove home. That evening we went back to church in a banged up car. A rolled over car wouldn't stop Dad from going to church.

Some of our Sunday afternoons were spent playing softball, riding bicycles, hiking through grain fields and in the wintertime we played in the snow with sleds and skis and made snow houses. We would dig caves out of huge snow piles. We had a lot of fun playing on high straw piles made by the threshing machine during harvest. Dad had built a sheep barn by putting poles in the ground, over laying the poles with fence wire and chicken netting, then threshing straw over top making a huge big straw pile to keep the sheep warm during lambing time. We often played on and rolled off the straw.

In the winter time we would make ice for the next summer. We made a rectangular wall out of straw bails. Each day we poured water on top of water from the day before letting it freeze over night. We kept adding water each day until we had a four foot square cube of ice. The ice was then covered with straw, preferably flax straw, two or three ft. deep. In the summer time we would go chop off a chunk of ice when needed. We needed ice to make homemade ice cream, this was a big hit in summer time.

In later years, in Florida, you often found Dad and Mom sitting on a bridge, with their fish poles in hand, maybe one watching while the other one slept. Dad also enjoyed deep sea fishing. He mounted a few nice trophies.

Mom enjoyed playing table games with us boys or reading us stories. Seemed like most of her spare time was used up sewing and knitting. She had a knitting machine that could make gloves, mittens, socks and caps. Then of course, cooking for a large family took a lot of her time. She knew how to season food. Every thing always tasted good. In these days we always had a common drinking dipper for the whole family dipping water out of the same bucket, everyone drinking from the same dipper. Water was carried in from a well by the barn. We didn't waste water.

/ TWO /
EARLY TEEN YEARS

By the time I was 15 I had completed my one-year of high school. Dad gave all six boys each one year of high school and then had us stay home to help on the farm. I got room and board (Mom's good cooking) and a car to drive to necessary things, but no wages. All six boys worked at home until they were 21 years old. Dad, having a large farm, always had hired men. This made opportunity to have fun and enjoy working.

As I said earlier, Adam and Ezra got to drive tractors so Paul and I drove horses. Driving horses was much different then driving a tractor, all you do is hit the starter and away you go. First of all the horses needed breakfast, a bucket of oats or ground up mixed feed. Now they needed a drink of water, the only water they got till noon, five hours later. Now you curry the horse down by brushing and raking his fur and relaxing his muscles. Next you began installing the collar, and then the harness, and last of all, the bridle. Now you do this four or six times and finally you have a team ready for work. Then you need to hook them up to a piece of equipment. There is a steering pole to hitch to the collar of the two horses in the middle. You still have the tugs, two on each horse, left to fasten to the evener of various styles on the equipment. Now if the flies weren't too bad that the horse didn't step over the tug and you had the reins in your hand you are ready to go. I did harrowing, plowing, seeding, mowing and raking hay, plus, cutting wheat with binder and four horses. There were times when farmers would hook as many as twelve horses together to pull one disc or plow or cultivator, hooked in tandem, six in front of the other six.

My horse driving experiences were not very good. With five horses on the harrow I had to walk behind all day long for many 10 hour days. The horses knew I was a kid and I just couldn't make them go fast enough. Dad would come out to the field and he could really get them going so fast, I had to run to keep up. Then when he left the field the horses slowed way down again. Dad would say, "Get'em goin," but I couldn't. When I had horses on the mower, I stopped to clean the sickle. Just then the horses stepped forward making the sickle move and cut a piece of my thumb out. I was about one mile from home, but just across from Art Tangelien's, our neighbor's house. They telephoned my parents who came and got me and patched up my thumb. Many a time I had runaways with the hay rake and bundle wagon. The horses would just take off.

MIRACLE 4 The summer I was 15, Dad thought I was a reliable driver. He bought a new John Deere binder pulled by four horses to cut wheat and make bundles for threshing. Dad sent me out about a mile away with the outfit. I was going along pretty good. I got off the binder to put on a chain that had slipped off. All of a sudden, something scared the horses and they took off as fast as they could pull the binder. Of course the binder was set in the motion position, as the horses ran faster all the moving parts like the sickle, gears, chains, and the big reel that pushed the grain onto the platform, these parts got into high velocity speed, throwing some off and breaking others. There was only one problem and that was the gate they went through, going home, wasn't wide enough. The horses got through, but the poor new binder hooked on the big corner post and busted everything in pieces. The horses broke loose and went home on a dead gallop.

When Dad saw the horses come home he wondered what

might have happened to me. Did I get run over? Was I still alive or was I cut in pieces? Dad and Mom both came out to meet me and needless to say, I never saw them happier. They weren't concerned about the binder, just happy to know that I didn't get a scratch. It was a miracle I was standing behind the machine when the horses took off.

As time went on the horse farming disappeared and Dad bought more tractors. One time he had five Case tractors, each one a different model to fit a particular job. Two of our cousins were from Brinsmade. They would come out to play with us and help work if Dad needed help. Dad put one of the boys on a tractor to pull the disc. It had no carriage wheels and therefore going in and out of the fields the disc blades rolled on the ground in a neutral position, not cutting or disturbing grass or soil. The driver forgot to change the angle of the blades when he got to the field and drove over the entire field, doing absolutely no good. We teased him about that.

The other boy was sent out to harrow a field that was planted to wheat. The wooden boss harrow laid flat on the ground. We started him out at four miles an hour, he maintained that speed till he finished the field, not knowing you don't go any faster coming back to the farm with that type of equipment. He put the tractor in road gear, 15 miles an hour. Dirt and rocks and wood filled the air, the harrow got a ride of a lifetime.

One young man came up from Jamestown to work for a week. The second day as he brought the tractor in from the field, from work, he forgot to slow the tractor down as he approached the yard and ran over the big upright gas pump. Knocked it down, breaking it off, flat to the ground. Dad said, "that is city guys for you".

By the end of this summer, in time to haul the wheat bundles in to thresh out the grain and put the straw up in big stacks, Dad made me machine oiler, greaser, light maintenance and belt tightener man. The equipment in those days didn't have sealed grease bearings, and therefore needed oil and grease every hour. This was a great move up for me and I really liked it. Kind of got me started on a route towards the new methods of combines that were just emerging at that time. Working with Dad around the thresher gave me good mechanical experience. The switch from threshing to combining had not taken place yet. Dad was determined at that time he never would make the change.

Harvest and threshing was always an exciting time of the year. It was a time when everybody could get involved in kind of a fun time. For one thing, you were never alone to do the work. Binding the grain into bundles and then standing the bundles on end to make a shock always took two to four people to do the work. It took six bundle teams to bring in the shocked grain to the thresher. It was a time of year when our cousins from Indiana would come out to help work. Cousins like Jessie Liechty, Robert Liechty, Ralph and Delilah Seiler, Velma and Dutch Klauffenstein, Bill Witmer, Merle and Eddie Neuhauser would all get involved.

There was never a dull moment with all these guys. When it rained, they tried to ride and break horses or fix up old cars. One rainy day when we couldn't thresh, Jessie saddled up one of Dads horses. This horse had never been ridden, was wild and rough to handle. Jessie was the star of the show. That horse bucked up and down, two feet off the ground. Jessie hung on to the end, the horse quit bucking, and became a nice riding horse.

Threshing time got Mom involved too. We had 10 to 12 hired men to make a full crew. Mom had to work very hard to feed the men and us boys. She always had a hired girl, Violet Palmer

Abrahamson, to help her. Violet was hard working and a great friend of the family. She fit in very well. She helped Mom 18 to 20 years. Some of us boys always helped Mom as well and it was long hours. Dad was a custom thresher. In other words, he moved the thresher from one neighbor to the next to thresh their grains. Sometimes they moved a cook car along and made meals out in the field. That old 1928 4 door sedan Buick was the main transportation for Mom and Violet to go from home base to the cook car or the field with coffee and lunches. The cook car, on wheels, was equipped with a stove, a sink, a water tank and a table long enough to seat 15 to 20 people. It had no refrigerator. I don't know how they kept food from spoiling. The cook car was moved from one work site to another with a team of horses or hooked onto the steam threshing rig. Threshing with a steam engine took a lot of man power. You needed a water boy and a man to keep the burner full of straw or coal. Dad had two steamers for farm work. I remember trying to plow with a steam engine pulling an eight bottom plow. The plow was put in and out of the ground by hand, two gangs on one lever. You needed two men on the plow just for that. The engine needed a fireman and a water boy. Traveling only three miles an hour you didn't get much plowed in a day. It was a sweet sound to hear that steamer CHOG A HOO--, CHOG A HOO--, CHOG A HOO.

    Before I leave this time of my life, I want to talk about our family life. We were definitely raised in a Christian home. As early as I can remember, going to church twice on Sunday and Bible study Wednesday nights, was a must. And then any revival or evangelistic meetings, within a 100 mile radius, had to be explored also. There were monthly fellowship meetings with other churches from a large area that we took in. We would even sing quartet songs at those meetings. Dad, our pastor Herman Kessler, Ezra and I were called quite often to sing. Our Mother played the piano. Then there was a small church, Christian Missionary Alliance at Brinsmade, where Ezra and I sang with George Herman Jr. and our Uncle Adam Witmer, Moms brother, in a quartet. We sang at public school programs, PTA and youth programs.

Go to church Sunday.
Sing in a choir.
Always accept an outstretched hand.
Rekindle old friendships.
Stop blaming others.
Wear polished shoes.
                              Life's little instructions.

A highlight for us boys was the summer family Bible Camp at Lakewood Park, (near Devils Lake city and on Devils Lake proper) North Dakota. This camp began back in 1935 or 1936. If we stayed overnight, we slept in tents, sleeping bags and blankets. Washrooms and bathrooms were not the greatest. In early 1940-45, Dad and Mom ran the camp store that had all kinds of groceries, ice cream and pop. Coming out of the 1930s Great Depression we had very little ice cream and candy. This was our chance to make that up. Paul and I were able to help at the store and we really had fun with that. It helped us get acquainted with lots of young people. One bad thing was camp only lasted two weeks each summer and we wanted more, especially when we got old enough to drive Dad's new cars and fill them up with girls and some boys. I well remember being jealous of the Herman Johnson boys. They were sons of the Superintendent of the North Dakota District of the Assemblies of God. These boys got first pick of the girls. The rest of us got girls after them. One night we had a load of mixed kids, I was driving 50 miles an hour, someone reached over and turned off the ignition key, when they turned it back on, the muffler was over loaded with gas, it exploded and made a big hole in the muffler of Dads new Plymouth car.

Dad had some trouble at camp meetings with us boys. Always some one of us boys would be missing when it was time to go home. We always went back to the farm at night, 25 miles away. One night one of us boys was missing too long so Dad said we'd go home without him. He started walking home. I'm sure Dad never slept that night. Adam got up and went to meet him about half way home at 9AM. Those girls were always chasing us boys, at least that is what we told Mom and Dad.

Before I leave this part I want to say that every morning at breakfast Dad would read a chapter out of the Bible and pray. It didn't matter how many men were sitting around the table. They had to listen till Dad was done before they could eat. Some of these fellows came into town riding on top of a train of boxcars, they were classified as bums, they slept out in the haybarn. A few fellows thought it was too much religion and quit on the job. However, some of the fellows liked our way of doing things and would come back year after year for harvest season. I remember Louis coming back many years, Herman was another one. And then there was Criss Graber, he got mad at Ezra. Criss was a slow driver in his automobile. One time Ezra took dads car and pushed Criss's car faster on the road. Criss up and left the farm.

MIRACLE 5 Dad and Mom always prayed for us boys. When Paul contacted scarlet fever, he was deadly sick and had such a high fever. He could easily have had brain damage or even died. I saw Dad and Mom go to Paul's bed and pray over him. The fever left and he began feeling better each day.

MIRACLE 6 In my case, I had gotten overheated in the school gym, went out in cold weather, cooled off too fast and contracted inflammatory rheumatism. The doctor said I had done damage to my heart. Mom put me in a special bed in our living room where I lay several days. The doctor said I would be laid up for six months. Dad and Mom began praying for me and in two weeks I was out of bed, and back to school within a month. The doctor said at that time I would never be any good for the Army. He was proven wrong several years later.

Dad and Mom were very reserved around us boys. I never saw them hug or kiss in my whole life. We don't know what went on in the bedroom. We boys often asked how they came up with six boys and a girl. I always felt loved at home. Dad thought the word LOVE sounded fresh, today we use the term sexy. My Dad never told me he loved or liked me, but I never got a spanking from my Dad or Mother. Mom played games with us, but Dad was always busy writing or reading. He sat at a desk, in front of the east window of the living room, by the hour. He would design wall mottos, gospel tracts, and stamps and stickers to put on envelopes. He spent a lot of time preparing sermons in case the opportunity came by.

I don't remember ever being short of food, even in the depression of the 30s. We always had good meals and Mom made lots of variety of foods. If mom wanted chicken for dinner we took a string and the hatchet, went to the chicken coop, picked out a chicken, tied a string around its neck, mom would hold the legs and the wings of the bird. I pulled the string with one hand and cut off its head with my other hand. After the chicken was done flopping around we put him in scalding hot water and picked off the feathers We had a big garden and 20 milk cows. Once a year Dad loaded up wheat from the bin, went to town and ground our own wheat at the mill for flour. We also had a 50-gallon barrel of frozen fish. No kidding, each winter Dad would buy a big 50-gallon barrel of Northern Pike fish that we could eat all winter with home canned vegetables and we also had home canned meats. By spring, the fish were all gone. We ate homemade cheese, popcorn and homemade ice cream all year long. We never went to bed hungry. Mom had a large swing table in the basement suspended from the ceiling by wires. This was a mouse free table where she stored cheese, cakes, pies and other good stuff. They also kept a year supply of potatoes in the basement. A good portion of our diet was corn meal mush. Mom cooked it like hot cereal for the evening meal, put some of it into bread loaf pans, let it set over night to stiffen, then slice and fry it for breakfast, man was it good with gravy or maple syrup and maybe both.

Dad always wanted running water, he worked at it until he finally had six boys running after water from the barn to the house.

Behind our house we only had half neighbors, only the top half. There were no doors between, we only saw them through the windows. We thought they were busts.

On June 6, 1940, our Dad turned 50 years of age. We had a large celebration. Neighbors from the Brinsmade Christian and Missionary Alliance Church and members of the Minnewauken Union Gospel Tabernacle, including Pastor Herman Kesler, all came to the 50 year event. We made two large freezers of homemade ice cream. There were cakes, pies and sandwiches. It just seemed like Dad was really old. Wow, 50 years and I was 14 at that time. As a boy, Dad looked old to me. I never ever saw our Dad use tobacco or alcoholic beverage.

Drafted into regular Army February 6, 1945

/ THREE /
COLLEGE DAYS AND ARMY LIFE

At age 16 1/2, in January 1943 I went to Minneapolis and enrolled at North Central Bible College. Back at that time colleges took students without a high school diploma. My brother Ezra was there in his senior year. I enjoyed this time in college, although beginning at the middle of the year I felt a little lost among a group of 400 students.

It was easy to make friends. We went out on weekends to various churches to help with meetings and to sing in groups from school. When I was in school, classes only went to noon. I got a job for afternoons working for the Minneapolis Street Car Company. My job was to be detective and watch how the conductors did business. Each streetcar had a driver and a conductor who would collect money when people got on to ride. I would get on and ride as a regular passenger and watch if the conductor put the people's money in the jar or if he stuck some in his pocket. I also reported how courteous he would be. It was fun. I'd get on at a certain point and ride 20 to 40 minutes, get off, and walk a few blocks to another route and go that way to some other point in town.

In those days there were 5¢ hamburgers and a bowl of baked beans for 5¢ at the White Castle. Everything else being equal I enjoyed Minneapolis.

Ezra graduated from North Central Bible College that spring, married a classmate, Marguerite Edlund, and left home to go farming on his own. Adam went to live with his uncles and aunts in Indiana, leaving me the oldest one to help Dad on the farm. I never went back to school. I stayed home and helped Dad on the farm. The winter of 1944 was interesting, Mom and Dad hooked to their camper and drove to Orange, Texas. This was the second camper that Dad built. It had more style and aero-dynamics than the first one he built. Paul, Silas, Reuben, and me, were along on the trip as well.

Second camper Dad built, spent winters of 41-42 in Orange, Texas. Dad worked in ship yards, I worked at gas station and grocery store.

MIRACLE 7 September 8th, 1943 my brother Adam was drafted into the US Army. He was married to Marcella, they had their first child, Anita. Adam was in the roughest of battles including the Battle of the Bulge. He had several narrow escapes, one of which I would like to include here and he quotes; "The time I believe our answer to prayer was most evident, was during the battle of the bulge. We had set up our command post in the basement of a house. The company commander came to me and said, we are completely surrounded by the German Army and unless God helps us we are doomed. Then the commander said, I have seen you read your Bible, would you read something and have prayer asking God to help us. Adam said sure, I would be glad to do that. He opened to the 91st Psalm, verses 7and 8 says, a thousand shall fall at thy side and ten thousand at thy right hand, but it shall not come nigh thee. Only with thine eyes you will behold and see the reward of the wicked. After reading this entire Psalm and having prayer it seemed the shelling ceased. I don't know why, except for prayer, a few hours later all 35 men in that basement got out of there alive. The rest of our Company of 250 men, in other basements, were either captured or killed. Only the 35 men in that basement got out of there alive. You can say what you want, but I believe God heard and answered our prayer that day." The Testament Adam read from that day was given to him by a Gideon at the induction center. Adam received both a Bronze Star and the Purple Heart for outstanding service.

It is the VETERAN who serves under the flag.
It is the VETERAN, not the preacher,
Who gives us freedom of religion.
It is the VETERAN, not the reporter,
Who has given us freedom of the press.
It is the VETERAN, not the poet,
Who has given us freedom of speech.
It is the VETERAN, not the campus organizer,
Who has given us freedom to assemble.
It is the VETERAN, not the lawyer,
Who has given us the right to a fair trial.
It is the VETERAN, not the politician,
Who has given us the right to vote.
It is the VETERAN, who salutes the Flag.

Dad tried to get a farm deferment from the military for me in the summer of 1944 but the draft board said Dad still had three more sons at home. I was drafted into the regular Army on February 6, 1945.

I had my basic training at Fort Lewis, Washington. Fort Lewis is one of the older camps in the country that had been fixed up real nice. We had good warm barracks to sleep in. Training grounds were good. Temperatures in the summer time were cool for drill practice and 10 to 20 mile hikes. At this particular time the United States was drafting men up to 45 years of age, many with families at home. Some of the guys were too heavy while others had bad feet and knees. When these guys were on long hikes they just couldn't make it. Ambulances followed us to pick up the fallouts.

While in boot camp I met Marvin Clarkson, who became a life long friend. We normally had Saturday and Sunday off unless we were on K.P. Marvin and I would travel to Christian Service Men's Centers. There was one in Seattle and one in Tacoma. These were real good places for clean young soldiers to go. They had beds for over night and lots of finger food, which was all free. They had Christian movies and we could sign up to do church projects if we wanted to go.

One weekend we tried hitchhiking to Caldwell, Idaho, which was Marvin's hometown. He said he knew a girl there I should meet. This was on a holiday so we had a three-day pass. We planned one day going, one day there and one day back. It didn't work. We got half way there by noon the second day and decided we had better head back. Connections for hitchhiking were no good that weekend. We got back early in the morning just in time to stand reveille.

When springtime came they moved me to Battalion headquarters up at Hamburg, Germany. My assignment was still the same upon arrival. Being there a few days our company commander, a captain, had a jeep that the mechanics of the motor pool could not get to start or run. One day the captain said he was going to Quarter Master to get a different jeep. They didn't have one for him, but while he was gone, only my third day there, I took an open end and box end wrench and readjusted the tappet setting on the valves of the engine and the motor started right up. Luckily, I had seen this done back home on the farm. When he came back and saw his jeep running, he was one happy captain. The next week I was promoted to the truck shop and received my first rank promotion to Private 1st Class, my first stripe on my sleeve.

I got along well with my commanders and life was pretty easy.
Strive for excellence, not perfection.
Think big thoughts but relish small pleasures.
Watch a sunrise at least once a year.
Never waste an opportunity to tell someone you love them.
Have a firm handshake.
Don't expect life to be fair.
Life's Little Instructions

Jon and Marvin Clarkson
Army Buddies

MIRACLE 8 The social part of army life was the toughest to put up with. Peer pressure was great. In Germany we stayed in big old houses, several guys in one room on single bunk army beds. I didn't like going out at night with the guys. Most all of them got drunk every night. I went to some shows and circus events with guys but stayed in most of the time. We all had pistols or revolvers in our footlockers. These were guns we bought off German people who needed money to live on. The guys were all good to me when they were sober. One night Tucker came home half drunk and got mad because I didn't go out with the guys. I was lying in bed. He took his pistol out of the footlocker and came over to me. He asked "Are you better than the rest of us?" holding the loaded pistol over my head, swearing at me and saying if I moved one inch he was going to shoot me! This lasted for 15 to 20 minutes,(seemed like an hour). I could easily have come home in a coffin. His gun was loaded and I knew it. My mother must have been home praying. I didn't move, I hardly breathed. One of the other guys came and got him away from me.

"My son, listen and accept my words and they will
multiply the years of your life. I have taught you
the way of wisdom, I have guided you along decent paths"
(Proverbs 4:10).

MIRACLE 9 Hitler had taken all the morality out of the German girls. They were taught to be used and abused by men any way a man wanted to do. There were always German girls hanging around our rooms. One girl, I don't even remember her name, got into bed with me four nights in a row. Mom must have really been praying. I can truthfully say that I never touched her. The guys would ask each morning, "Did you make out?" She gave up on me and moved in with another guy. Later, he went to the clinic and discovered he had VD (venereal disease). Most of those girls were carrying diseases.

One night I was in bed. Beds were close together and a girl was in bed with another man next to mine. After that man went to sleep the girl reached in my bed and attempted to focus on my private parts. I got out of there and never saw her again.

The boat ride coming back from Europe was different than going over. No more big high bunk beds in the bottom of the boat and none of that seasick stuff. Because of the Army promotions up to Tec/Sgt (five stripes) I was offered a private room on the ship coming back. It was a small room but nice. Our meals were better. I ate with the commissioned officers. In this private room I had time to read and think of where my life was going. If I had any touch of salvation in Christ, I know I had lost it all by this time. The army life had gotten the best of me. I was miserable inside and did not want to go home that way. I did not want to disappoint my mother who had prayed for me every day I was gone.

He paid a debt He did not owe
I owed a debt I could not pay,
I needed someone
To wash my sins away.

MIRACLE 10 GREATEST OF ALL I made an altar by my bedside, knelt and gave my heart to Jesus. This was a new life experience. I came away from this altar, washed by tears of repentance. I felt so clean and new. I just knew life had a new feeling. Everything looked brighter and the load of guilt was gone. I had a new friend in Jesus. I can't explain it fully, but it is wonderful. If you haven't tried it, you are missing the best part of life. You really need to try it, you can talk to Jesus just like another real person.

And now I sing a brand new song
Amazing grace;
Christ Jesus paid the debt
That I could never pay.

The first thing I did was clean up my duffle bag. A friend had given me part of a bottle of liquor. I never drank any of it. Don't really know why I kept it so long. Also had a carton of cigarettes that I had gotten through trading with other soldiers that needed money for their gambling. I never smoked any of that carton either. I'll never forget the day I walked to the edge of that ship, looked at the big blue ocean, waves fifty feet high, and threw them both overboard. It was ironic to have sins forgiven crossing the Atlantic Ocean. I found the Lord at sea level, 0 degrees altitude. Like the song goes, "my sins are buried in deepest sea, my sins are blotted out I know."

"You will tread our sins underfoot,
and hurl all our iniquities into the
depths of the sea" (Micah 7:19).

This confession took away all desires for either drinking or smoking. It was part of the clean-up from my altar experience. I am convinced every person needs his or her own private altar experience. You need to get down on your knees and talk to Jesus like you would talk to your best friend in your home, tractor, truck, or where ever. Jesus is a real person and you will know when you have gotten his attention.

"Blessed is the one who is always
fearful of sin. But whoever is hard-
hearted falls into disaster" (Proverbs 28:14).

I have sat with many professional people in large conventions and political rallies where liquor was free, but it has never tempted me in the least. In my army life I saw what alcohol could do to people. There are many guys I've seen beaten up in fights all because they drank too much, got too loud for their own good, or had their noses broken because they got kicked in the face. I've seen it all.

"Wine makes people mock, liquor makes them noisy, and everyone under their influence is unwise" (Proverbs 20:1).
Oh! What a Savior, Oh! Hallelujah.
He gave his life blood for even me.

Marvin P. Dalton

/FOUR/
BACK TO THE FARM

In the spring of 1947 I went back to Brinsmade to work on the farm for Dad and Mom. The summer of 47 I turned 21. Dad said I could farm on my own the next year, 1948. I made plans to do that. I had some G.I. money coming to go to school, so decided to take one more year of high school at Leeds, North Dakota. This was the fall, winter and spring of 47-48. I really enjoyed high school bookkeeping and also took physics and took typing class. I got straight A's, although I don't know how I did it. That winter I stayed with Uncle Mike and Aunt Martha O'Connell.

Become the most positive and enthusiastic person you know.
    Ask for a raise when you feel you have earned it.
    Return a borrowed vehicle with the gas tank full.
    Buy whatever kids are selling in their front yard.
    Feed a stranger's expired parking meter.
    Say "thank you" a lot, say "please" a lot.
    Leave the toilet seat in the down position.
    Put your tissue into the trash.
                   Life's Little Instruction

At this time in my life I began observing two young farmers in our neighborhood. Jim and Joe were cousins to each other. Jim took over his dads well established farm. I remember him driving by our Dads farm many times, to check on hired help he had in his farming operation, which included the farm right south of ours that Dad had to give up in the dirty thirties. Jim also had a custom harvesting operation and an airplane to fly to Kansas and Oklahoma to check on his harvest operation. Jim bought new cars, trucks, and equipment all of the best. An interesting note here was the fact that Jim also farmed the bottom land of Devils Lake, where he grew flax several years. Now Devils Lake is the largest lake in North Dakota and probably in the entire Northwest. Jim also was a popular figure in civic and political circles.

Joe came from a poor family home, his dad was an alcoholic. Joe started farming by renting 80 acres of ground. He rented used small equipment and worked hard, doing his own work, to get started.

I kept thinking, if I could only find myself somewhere in between Jim and Joe, thinking I would probably never own a combine, and for sure not an airplane, but I started and as time went on you will see.

Nineteen forty-eight was to be my first year of farming. Dad gave me 480 acres to farm. Dad sold me one of his tractors, a D-Case, and let me use his equipment to get started. In turn, I did seeding and work for him. This Case tractor was different than today. No cab, no heater and no air. The tractor was known as a plow tractor. That meant the tractor would follow a furrow made by the plow. We would be plowing late in the fall, sometimes we even plowed down fresh snow. Then it was cold on the tractor and we would get off and run to keep warm or we would run and catch baby rabbits. Sometimes we picked up stones to throw at birds or gophers. We did all these things while the tractor and plow were moving down the field.

I went to the bank, where Dad and Ezra banked, to borrow money for farming. The banker, Vic Helberg, asked what I had for collateral and "I said, nothing." He said, "on the performance of your dad and brother, Ezra," he would loan me enough to buy seed and fertilizer and some spray. Ezra was established in farming by this time and he helped me too. So with $3,000 borrowed money and no equity I was able to seed my first crop of wheat.

By this time I knew I needed help from a better source if I was going to succeed. One Sunday afternoon in June of 1948 I took a walk down a path to one of my fields. I prayed all the way out and back asking the Lord for his help and guidance. In return I vowed to give to churches 10% and another 10% to missions of any profits I made. This was not an ordinary walk. I felt a real closeness to Jesus and a lifted spirit because I knew I had made an agreement with God. I have never forgotten that special day.

"Trust in the Lord with all your heart,
do not rely on your own understanding.
In all your ways acknowledge him, and
he will make your path smooth" (Proverbs 3:5-6).

When harvest time came that year, Dad, who was a custom thresher, harvested my crop. The crop was good that year. We had rain enough to produce a twenty bushel wheat crop, wheat was three dollars a bushel, the same price as it is today, but our costs were only 10 percent of what they are now. It gave me a good start for another year. Uncle Mike gave me his land to farm in 1949 so then I had 640 acres to farm.

The year 1949 offered a new experience. Ezra and I bought a used self-propelled combine and a used International truck. We loaded the combine on the truck and went to Kansas to harvest wheat. We did this in 1949-50. In 1951 Dad bought a combine and went with us to Kansas. Prior to this time dad thought everything had to be put in bundles and threshed. It was hard for him to give up a system that had worked, probably since the beginning of time. When he saw how easy it was for us boys to harvest, it didn't take long for him to change systems. I can remember just before harvest in 1950 I had been looking at a new system of putting grain

Our first coop used combine and used 1946 INT Truck loaded for Kansas 1949. First service truck was a two wheel trailer.

into the farm bin. Up to this point everything was shoveled off by hand with a scoop shovel. Larson Implement was introducing a new grain auger where you just dumped the grain out of the back of the truck and the auger took it into the bin. If you had a hoist on the truck you could lift that and the grain would flow into the auger. One day I came home with hoist on my truck and a grain auger behind. My Dad said, "Jonathan, don't buy everything you see up town, your going to go broke".

In 1950 Dad bought the John Deere business in Leeds. Dad had traded one of his farms to Mr. Hobson when buying the business in Leeds. Then in 1951 I got to farm the Hobson land, giving me another 480 acres to farm.

MIRACLE 11 One interesting side note during 1949-1950, I had been dating Delores Herman. It seems as though I won her parents more than Delores. We never really did hit if off too good. Her parents thought I was okay. Mr. George Herman offered to sell me one of his farms. This was the first chance I had to buy real estate, and what a deal he gave me! I didn't have to pay anything down and only paid 4% interest, and no real due date. You can see I didn't get the daughter but instead I got the farm.

MIRACLE 12 Having started farming and raising cattle, the Minnewauken School System conducted Ag-shop classes for farmers who wanted to learn welding or build small tools, etc. While I was feeding baled hay, I thought I should make a bale hook. This was a hand held hook to pick up 50 lb. bales and place them out for cattle to feed on. The hook was all completed except to grind off the rough edges. As I was grinding, the hook caught on the grind wheel. It threw the hook right at my head, cutting off the top of my ear, went through my skull, and gave me a fractured skull. I was knocked out and down on the floor. A schoolmate and friend of mine, Don Herman, was there and picked me up, put me in his new Chevrolet car and hauled me to Devils Lake Hospital. Was I ever surprised to wake up in that place. Lying there five days, thinking and praying, a white figure came and stood at the end of my bed. It was either my guardian angel or Jesus. I prefer to think it was the latter. A healing took place and I had no bad effects from the accident. P.T.L.

Now back to farming, looking back at my walk down the path to a field of mine, my salvation experience in the ship and the accelerated start in farming, it showed me the Lord had good things in store for me.

"Trust in the Lord with all thine heart and
lean not on thine own understanding.
In all thy ways acknowledge Him and He shall
direct thy path" (Proverbs 3:5-6).

MIRACLE 13 One summer day there was one bad episode.

Ezra was out in a pasture fixing fence where he had cows and a bull. I just happened to stop by when I saw the horned bull chasing him. I put the truck in high gear and set out to help. Just in time, I got the truck between him and the bull and pushed the bull over the fence. Nobody knows what could have happened had I not been there. Bulls are known to win that type of battle.

"The name of the Lord is a strong tower a righteous person runs to it and is safe" (Proverbs 18:10).

By this time farming seemed to be my nitch. I was renting more land and bought a second half section, was doing more combining and in the year 1951 I also helped Dad run the Ford business in Leeds. I didn't care much for that type of business. Seemed people were hard to satisfy. Retailers, you have my sympathy.

ROMANCE At age 26 August 1952 I decided to go visit my brother Paul and his wife Jean at Kulm, ND where he was the youth paster at the Assembly of God Church. Going to Church twice that Sunday I decided to ask the young piano player FERN JOHNSON if she would like a ride home. She said "yes" and we were off to a good start. About the same time my brother Silas started dating MARTHA PELTZ. In the summer of 1953 there were two weddings, Silas and Martha on June 7th and Fern and I on June 9th. We were two happy couples.

BUILDING A BUSINESS The years 1953-1956 rolled along fast. We got into a pattern where I was farming and helping some at Dad's John Deere and Ford business and Fern was doing bookkeeping for Dad at the stores. Farming was growing and I continued the southern harvest combining. Dad and Mom went combining three years and they took Frank Harris along. He talked

Our wedding picture June 9, 1953

a lot and would get up on his knees in bed and wave his hands and argue. It was always an interesting sight. Fern and I also chose help like Earl Loken, Wayne Rolle, Darwin Verke and others. We had a travel trailer along where Fern and the children could spend time during the days and make noon and early evening lunches. The men stayed in motels. Fern was great at cooking and making lunches as we traveled from one job to another. Fern didn't really like it, especially the severe thunderstorms in Kansas. The thunder was so loud it really shook that little camper we had. Fern would grab me and ask, "Are we okay, Jon?"

Back at home, Silas was working for Dad at the John Deere store and trying to find his place in life. Silas and Martha had an invitation to go to Jamestown as associate pastor in 1955. I thought this was the end of our farming and business as partners. One thing we claimed early in our business life was the 1st Psalm:

"Blessed is the man who does not walk in the counsel
of the wicked or stand in the way of sinners or sit in the
seat of mockers. But his delight is in the law of the
Lord, and on his law he meditates day and night. He is
like a tree planted by the water, which yields its fruit in
season and whose leaf does not wither. Whatever he
does prospers. Not so the wicked! They are like chaff
that wind blows away. Therefore the wicked will not
stand in judgment, nor sinners in the assembly of the
righteous for the Lord watches over the way of the
righteous, but the way of the wicked will perish"
(Psalm 1:1-6).

By this time Fern had decided to earn some cash of her own. She took an office job working for Ezra who was running Dad's John Deere store. Nineteen fifty-five was a good year for farming.

Fern needed a better car to drive to work, so we bought a new 1956 two-door hard top Fairlane Ford. What else could we buy when Dad was selling Fords? This was good for Fern. She got out of the house more and felt more needed. Ezra began working for Dad at John Deere and I took over some of his farming.

In 1956 Silas and Martha drove up from Jamestown to visit us and have dinner. They also asked Fern and me to come to Jamestown to look at a farm that was for sale. I told Fern we could probably take off a day and go but was sure nothing would come of it. It so happened we stayed the second day and bought a nice 960-acre farm, jointly half and half with Si and Martha.

There was a renter on there for that year and in 1957 and in 1958 we were able to get Edwin and Luella Nitschke to move on the farm and help us. This farm was the headquarter site of an operation called "The Chicago Ranch", Owned by Chicago investors.

A little background of how we got started in the mobile homes business might be helpful. While Silas and Martha moved to Jamestown to work in the church, he also had to make a living. Having connections with Dad's franchise at Leeds, he could get a mobile home at factory cost. He bought one to live in. While living in it he advertised it for sale. The home sold quickly and they drove to the factory with their Mainline Ford car and got a second new home. Advertising it again, it sold quickly. Off to the factory for the third home. This was repeated five or six times. It was time to go into a full-time business selling mobile homes.

Silas opened a sales lot on the south side of town. This was the beginning of Liechty Homes. Mr. Rabel sold him enough land to start a sales lot and a mobile home park. To sell mobile homes you need a place to park them. We did some planning, bought several acres from Mr. Rabel and built Holiday Park Village.

By this time Silas and I had been working and farming together and now had taken our brother Ezra in as a partner and our business will be referred to JES. In 1958 the Brown Farm came up for sale. JES managed to put money down and bought 480 acres adjoining our 960. Up to this time I had been banking at Minnewaukan Bank where I first started. I kept increasing my operating loans each year until the loans exceeded the banking limits. Mr. Helberg said, "Jon you're exceeding our banking limits, but we will still go with you. You are one of our biggest customers." I was glad for the reputation our dad and Ezra had built for me. Now to start farming in the Jamestown area, I needed a banker to help me there. I went to 1st National Bank and got turned down flat. The banker asked how many cattle I was going to have on the farm and I responded with " NONE." The banker said this was a cattle farm and they were not interested.

MIRACLE 14 Some years later, we did have cattle on this farm. But in the meantime I walked across the street to Jamestown National Bank and was introduced to Fritz Buegel. Mr. Buegel had just moved to the Jamestown Bank recently from a Cando bank. Now Cando was right close to our Brinsmade and Leeds area. Although we had never banked at Cando, Fritz knew our name and reputation. He gave me all the money I needed without a budget and continued that way getting up to six digit figure loans, as long as he was in the bank. I feel this banker was moved to Jamestown to help me. Praise the Lord.

"The fear of the Lord is the beginning
of knowledge. Stubborn fools despise
wisdom and discipline" (Proverbs 1:7).

Having gotten settled in the house on the farm I thought there must be mornings I could take an extra hour and sleep. Awaking, I might have prayed:

Dear God
So far today, I've done all right.
I haven't gossiped. .
I haven't lost my temper, I haven't
lied or cheated, I haven't been
greedy, grumpy, nasty, selfish or
over-indulgent. I am very
thankful for that. But, in a few
minutes, Lord, I'm going to get
out of bed, and from then on,
I'm going to need a lot more help. Amen.

This was also the year JES opened a sales lot for mobile homes in Bismarck. Marvin Eckman had been in training at the Jamestown office for two years. Marvin and Marjorie took the position there. It was great to have good honest reliable people in charge in Bismarck.

As we entered the 60s, the momentum really began to grow. In 1963 we began making plans to build a new house on the farm. Yes, we liked living out there well enough to build. We looked at plans and contacted builders and gave a contract in the fall of 1963 to Art Swanson.

We farmed that year and in the fall JES bought 1120 acres of the Henry Erickson farm. By this time we had acquired Ezra's 960 acre farm into the JES partnership. Now it was a challenge to upgrade and expand equipment to farm 4000 acres.

We were well settled in and enjoyed the winter sports of snow mobile riding until March of 1966 when a 3-day blizzard came upon us. We didn't go out of the house the last two days of the storm. We had 36 inches of snow with strong winds. The snow piled up very high, it made snow banks over the house, completely covering half of the house under the snow. We could walk on snow right over the house. There was enough snow to ride our snowmobiles over top of the house. We shoveled our way out of the house and into the farm shop to get a tractor out to open driveways and barns. We had no car garage. After the storm we couldn't find the car. I started digging down where I thought the car stood. Digging down 5 feet into the snow, I finally found the roof of our car. Clothes lines, garbage cans, and even the electric meter, were all covered up. It took two more days for roads to open up so the school bus could run and so we could get to town for mail and groceries.

We didn't know if we had any cattle left. They didn't get feed or water for three days. Fortunately, enough of the cattle survived in a huddle in the barn, but now we had to find feed for the cattle

House covered with snow March 1966

under all the snow.

Thou wilt keep him in perfect peace,
whose mind is stayed on thee:
because he trusteth in thee   (Isaiah 26:3).

April came, it warmed up, and the snow started to melt. Water ran all over the creek south of our house and flooded over. Finally it got dry enough so we could go farming again.

This same year, 1966, JES looked at plans to build Skyway Mobile Home Park in Bismarck. This would provide 400 spaces to sell and place homes in the capital city. Business was good in home sales, even if we didn't stay open for business on Sundays.

Remember the Sabbath day to keep it holy.
Six days shalt thou labour and do all thy work
                    (Exodus 20: 8-9).

MIRACLE 15 Next come Charles DeLair to sell us his farm. Let's go back to the beginning of this story. We had moved out to the farm back in 1961. The DeLair farm joined our farm on the south side. Each winter, northwest winds blew snow off our farm filling his yard with big piles of snow. We had been over there a few times for coffee. It was a pain to see him move all that snow out after every storm. One day we offered him to plant trees on our farm for a windbreak to stop this snow. He asked "Would you really let me do that?" We said, "Yes, go ahead and there's no charge for the ground." He planted about two acres of ground to trees. We were so surprised that only two years later Chuck DeLair offered to sell us his farm. He didn't advertise at all. He said he wanted us to have the farm. JES made the down payment and bought another 720 acres of the Old Chicago Ranch. It is surprising what a cup of cold water or a cup of hot coffee can do, returns were good this time.

After the sale, Chuck and Rita DeLair moved to Oregon. We remained friends, visiting them out west twice and they back here. Another DeLair family, Hank and Ruby, were close neighbors. Their children rode the school bus along with our children. When Hank decided to quit farming, back in the 70s, he asked a nephew, Frances Lee, to farm their 1000 acres of ground. These families have been great friends. We had the privilege of praying with Hank before he passed away. It is amazing how long friendships can last.

MIRACLE 16 After their nephew quite, we began farming the 1000 acre tract for Hank and Ruby back in the 80s, have farmed their place ever since and have a new contract this year for 2007, the time of this writing

We thank the Lord for blessing our cup of cold water to Mr. DeLair. We tried to be faithful in doing our part for the Lord. By now we were able to give 30% of our income to charity. We still took time to shut the farm down on Wednesday nights for Bible studies and took the children to church.

"The Lord is my Shepherd. I shall not want. He makes me lie down in green pastures. He leads me beside still waters. He restores my soul. He leads me in the paths of righteousness for His namesake. Even though I walk through the valley of the shadow of death, I will fear no evil, for you are with me. Your rod and staff, they comfort me"

(Psalm 23:1-4).

The Liechty Boys
Seated left to right: Jonathan, Adam, Ezra
Standing left to right: Reuben, Paul, Silas

/FIVE/
EXPANDING REAL ESTATE

If you remember earlier in the book I was watching Jim and Joe. Now I found two more model farmers I should observe. Bill and Ben were the two biggest farmers I knew, but wasn't always sure of their motives.

There were times in the late seventies and eighties when these two guys bought most all the farm real estate that came up for sale. They worked men and equipment as much as possible, they had no time for church on Sundays or Bible studies during the week. Seemed they could outbid anyone buying farm land. We bid against them one time, they blew us out of the water.

We went on a farm tour to Bills farm. They had a special barn for six of the biggest tractors you could buy and enough equipment to fill the whole farm yard.

Ben had 10 tractors, 10 planters, 10 cultivators and ten of each other thing he needed. Ben had airplanes, motor homes and fancy horse trailers. I thought they really knew something about farming that I didn't know. Seemed like nothing could ever stop Bill and Ben, I just kept watching.

In 1967, JES bought the 525 acre Mayer farm which laid on the banks of Beaver Creek. This farm had a good small house, barn and shop. One of our hired help and his family lived here. One spring beaver creek jammed up a big ice dam. When the ice let loose water flooded the entire valley where the house sat. The water picked up the house off the foundation and floated it down to the bridge at the Montpelier road. There it stood still a little bit, started swirling round and round with the water and disappeared down under the bridge, that water swirl must have completely dismantled that house, never to be seen again. This has been an interesting farm for sportsmen. A small creek runs the entire length of the farm, has lots of trees and high hill slopes to hunt on. All of our families have hunted there. The farm has drawn hunters all the way from Minnesota and Texas. The focal point of our hunting seems to be there. Over one half of our deer have been taken on this farm. Yet many deer have escaped, dogging our spray of bullets.

The Mayer farm always produced a lot of deer and good hunting.

In the 60s, Trinity Bible College was located in Jamestown. By this time we needed two full time employees on the farm plus extra summertime help. I never worried about workers. I said, "Lord, its yours, help me in ways to serve You and give to charities, church and missions," which has always been a big part of our giving. It so happened I've always had help on the farm.

Now Wesley Loven, who lived just two miles west and one/half south, our brother in law, had come on board for full-time employment. As I mentioned earlier, Gene and Shirley Wolff were living on the Everding farm and he was employed full time. For part-time help, we had students from Trinity, like Darryl Wileman, Bob Bachman and Allen Fercho who had farm backgrounds and could pitch right in. Darryl could see a problem and fix it. Bob was a good steady man, got a lot done, and Allen was OK too. Earl Fercho, Allens dad, came out a few days and adjusted our grain drill seeder.

One good man from Trinity Bible College was Mick Hessler. Mick did some scraper work for us with a six yard scraper and a 4020 John Deere tractor working in Jamestown and out on the farm. One day he got a little too aggressive and rolled over the scraper. No damage done, really, we set it back up and Mick kept on working.

We had one Trinity boy from New York City. He was a character. We brought him out from town Sunday night. When we got outside city limits he asked, "Where are the lights?" When he got out of bed Monday morning he asked, "Where are the houses?" He had never seen open range country. Then I told him to fill the grain seeder. He put fertilizer in the seed box and seed in the fertilizer box. To tell the truth, I don't think he knew what was seed and what was fertilizer. Then I put him on a tractor where he turned too short and bent the hitch. We took him back to town that night.

One day we had a bad windstorm. It blew the flax swaths and rolled them up into piles large enough to plug the feeder house on the combine. To harvest the flax, I went to Trinity, got four guys out and gave them each a pitchfork. I drove the combine from pile to pile and those guys forked in the flax. After two days of that they were glad we finished.

MIRACLE 17 It was one of these earlier years, probably 1968-1970 the Lord awarded me a new Ford pickup. I say that because there were times when money was short, we were maintaining our pledges to the missionaries, and yet it just seemed to work out that we could buy new vehicles as we needed them. We felt everything we possessed was a hand down from God. Driving out his new Ford I decided to go out in the country for a little drive. It was just before dark, got down the highway 15 miles and the new Ford stopped. It was 12 to 15 degrees below zero and I wasn't dressed heavy enough to start walking. If I sat there till morning I would have been a solid ice cube. Thank the Lord an Angel drove up in four door sedan, stopped and told me to get in. This Angel took me to my house, I got out, and it drove away never to see it again. Often we think Angels are only spiritual beings up in the clouds somewhere. We are made earthy and Gods hand can just as well be earthly too.

"Honor thy father and thy mother that thy
days may be long upon the land which
the Lord thy God giveth thee" (Exodus 20:12).

In May 1968, Bob and Sharon Unterseher graduated from Trinity. I had put a "help wanted" ad on the bulletin board of Trinity. Bob answered the ad, and right out of school we made a deal and he began a relationship that went far beyond that summer of work and is very current today.

On Christ, the solid rock, I stand;
All other ground is sinking sand.
        Edward Mote, 1863
No one can lay any foundation other than
the one already laid, which is Jesus Christ.
        1 Corinthians 3:11

"Jesus said, suffer the little children to
come unto me, and forbid them not for
of such is the kingdom of God" (Mark 10:14).

In 1970, a new idea came along. JES formed a partnership with Carl and Gertrude Mueller to build Kirkwood Apartments in Bismarck. Carl was to be the driving force. A total of 180 units were built on that property. Later on another piece of ground was converted to an additional 45 units.

By this time we were building Park Apartments in Jamestown, which ended up with 144 units. The Jamestown units were managed and operated by Wayne Monson.

Wayne and Carl were both very dedicated men. Carl was with us for 20 years, contracted cancer and passed away. Gertrude continued managment several more years. Wayne has been with us 34 years and retired in 2006 at age 80.

A friend and business partner of later years made a speech I haven't forgotten. Lloyd Hansen, having residences in Florida and Norway, and we have the privilege of serving on the Amity board together, talked about how important connections are and that the Lord keeps leading us to the right people. We need to be attentive to opportunities, but the Lord will lead us. That has surely been the case with Fern and I and also JES. If you notice as this story goes on we have been blessed many times over, by meeting the right people at the right time. There are many good connections yet to come.

"For I know the plans I have for you,
declares the Lord, plans to prosper you
plans to give you hope and a future"(Jeremiah 29: 11).

Through the years, Silas and I worked together the most.
Inside JES, Silas was a good connection for me. Although he

is sharper and quicker than me, we were always able to work and play together. We did many things together including flying our twin-engine airplane. We airlifted men and supplies to our South Dakota farm operation for three years, landing that twin engine airplane at Pierre, South Dakota many times. Our 1000-acre farm was only 20 miles east of Pierre.

In 1971, JES was able to buy the Schultz farm which consisted of 320 acres.

This was an interesting approach. Mr. Schultz said he had tried to sell the farm through the FHA and Bank Finance systems and nothing came together. I told him we would pay cash. He said we had more power than either of the other systems. Really, I think the Lord was just saving it for us.

One more time I had to think of my walk to the farm.

In 1972 we rented the Walter Piehl farm. This was a good 800-acre piece of ground. Walter had signed a five-year contract at $12.00 per acre, which was okay for then. Soon after signing this contract, land rents began to go up. I know Walter felt badly. I paid him extra money each year in accordance with the times. We created a friendship that has never quit. We farmed his farm for 30 years and enjoyed it. I never felt right taking advantage of them just because we had a five year contract. I am sure we wouldn't have had the farm for 30 years if I hadn't paid more than our contract called for. Walter and Hattie were great people. Every year or two they joined us at a steak house for dinner. Four different times we met in Mesa, Arizona, in the wintertime. What great camaraderie! Walter always paid, unless somehow I could sneak the ticket away from him. We had the pleasure of having them in our home also.

We were still sending combines south for the harvest in Kansas.

Some of the workers for a few years were Chris and Llewelyn Paulson. Chris was in his late 60s, but tough as nails. His son Llew was young and single, but got married and brought Betty along too. Then there was Lyle Vilhauer and Dan Rueb who both were good operators. The middle 70s is the time when Sherry and Jeff were the right age for harvest work. Jeffrey got an early start driving combine. At 12 years of age, I would let Jeff get into the cab of the combine. He knew how to start and stop the machine. If any little thing went wrong he was to toot the horn, never getting out to fix it. I was always near enough, it was a safe thing. Jeff's Mom didn't like the idea too well.

In Sherry and Jeffrey's Junior and Senior year, Fern and I loaded up the combines pulled by one truck each. Jeff and I each drove a truck pulling a combine on a trailer. Mom and the girls drove the new 4-door pickup with fuel tank and service supplies. Lyle Vilhauer was along as combine operator. Lyle and Jeff drove the combines, Sherry moved trucks in the field to keep up for filling with wheat, and I hauled the grain to town. Sherry seemed to catch on fast to truck driving. She wasn't afraid to push down the peddle and get things moving. It wasn't the best for Jeania, who was 8-10 years old. She broke out from wheat dust allergies. Mom was the morale builder with all the good sandwiches, snacks and pop.

The worst area for cutting wheat was around Kiowa, Kansas, where the soil below black topsoil was a yellow clay. It never failed that we would get a big cloudburst of rain. Trucks and combines both would sink in to the axles. When that clay dried it was on to stay. The farmer always kept a big farm tractor in the field to pull us out of the mud.

My memory fails me as to which two years we joined forces with Virgil Gerig to go combining. He had a semi-trailer that would haul two combines. He hauled one of our John Deere combines and I took the other with a single axle truck and trailer. Chris and Llew Paulson made both these trips along with Darwin Verke. These were pretty good years. Virgil had good large farm customers to cut for.

On one of these combine trips, pulling into Pratt, Nebraska, I stopped to go into a store to buy some socks. It was early in the morning, just as the stores were opening up for the day. I picked out the socks I wanted, paid the clerk, grabbed the package and went out to the field to combine. That evening we checked into our motel. My brother Paul, who was along on this trip, asked me what that bag of money was doing up on the back window of the car. I asked, "What bag?" Paul said, "There is a bag of money out there." Upon examining the bag, I found I had picked up the money bag the clerk had intended to put into the till. I went in the next morning and returned the money. As the merchant had no idea who I was or where I was working, he thought the money was gone. The merchant asked what he could do for me. I said, "Nothing, except maybe some popularity." Two days later this story came out over national news. My neighbor, George Herman Jr. up in North Dakota verified this. He had heard it on national news.

Around 1972, JES started building a park in Devils Lake. Taking farm tractors to start excavation of soil, Henry Rassmusen and Marvin Lee drove the 5020 tractors up to the site. Wesley Loven drove up the pickup with fuel and supplies. They worked every day except Sunday to get done before freeze up. After cutting through a twelve foot hill and moving one-half of it we got done in good time. We built 120 spaces there.

In 1974, we had a chance to trade in a farm on the purchase

of a mobile home. This was a 600-acre farm near Eureka, South Dakota. We rented out this farm to a local farmer. We later enrolled this farm into the government CRP program. JES also bought another 700 acres and rented 300 more at Blunt, South Dakota. We farmed there, moving equipment from our Montpelier farm. This was about the time that Jeff and Kenis Loven, Jeff's cousin, and Wesleys son, were old enough to drive tractors. They would start at 6 o'clock in the morning and before dark they would be down to Blunt, 250 miles from home. It sounds like a drag but listening to their stories, they killed gophers and birds and counted rabbits on the way.

One more big event took place in 1973. That Sunday school girl, Marilyn Johnson, whom we helped through Trinity Bible College, was ready to get married. While at college she met this Yakima Valley cowboy, Tim Waddington. We had heard about this after school started in August and on November 30th they were married. The wedding was nice. They were a good match for each other.

The Waddingtons were a musical family. Tim would take his guitar, play and sing, and always draw a crowd. After marriage, Tim felt a call of the Lord to get into some type of ministry. Coming from a family of 19 children, Tim always had brothers and sisters who would make up a musical team and travel through towns and churches, holding concerts and speaking. They did this for several years and then the children started coming. It was always a joy to have them pull into our yard and spend a day or two. One day Tim and Marilyn drove in with two of his sisters, Miriam and Carolina. The two girls went into our downstairs bedroom and slept all night and with no windows in the room they didn't realize time was going on. They missed breakfast and lunch, coming out of their room at four o'clock the next afternoon. It seemed funny at the time. We usually tried to feed them and fill their big bus gas tank before they left.

Finally the family got bigger, to a point, where they needed more room. Tim was able to buy a big diesel bus. It was interesting to fill that machine, 150 or more gallons at a time. He formed a board of directors and put me into one position on the board. Conrad Twedt also was on the board. We would meet at various places where Tim would minister and try to help. Tim and Marilyn believed that,

"God so loved the world that He gave His only
begotten Son that whosoever believed on Him
should not perish but have everlasting life" (John 3:16).

Taking used school buses and making them into Sunday school buses was all the rage in the 1970s. We had become friends with a school bus dealer in Fargo. He would sell us his used buses at reasonable prices. Now remember, we had our nephew, David Sjostrom, work for us summers while in college and now he was a pastor in the state of Washington.

David knew who needed buses. I would buy them in Fargo and find drivers to take them west and David would sell them out there. We never made much money but had reasons to drive out west to visit and help some churches. Bob Unterseher drove sometimes. One time we took three buses as far as a men's retreat in western Montana. Three men came from Washington and drove them the rest of the way. We always worked some fun around each trip. At this Montana retreat, there were hot springs of water so we would bathe in the pools and then take a roll out in the snow. Talk about anything crazy, we did it. We even sewed Bob's pajamas shut one time, among other crazy things.

One of four pink snoopy buses running for Sunday school while David and Connie were youth pastors in Jamestown.

Family pictures in early 70s.

77

/SIX/
BUSINESS AND TRAVEL

Another project of the middle 70s was building the Farm Pup Trailers. Back in those years most farm trucks were single axle trucks, which only allowed them to haul three to four hundred bushels of grain. I devised a hopper bottom trailer that hauled another 300 and 400 bushels along with the truck. It was like

Farm Pup trailer built to add payload behind a bobtail truck.

hauling two loads to the elevator in one trip.

The Farm Pup trailer seemed to catch on well and sales were increasing. We were building them in our farm shop. It was taking more shop room. We had hired two men as part-time welders. We asked ourselves, "Should we build another shop, and if so, on the farm or in town?" We had put out around 50 trailers and had a chance to sell our idea, our jigs, and drawings to a machine manufacturer in Fargo. We were to get royalties on each trailer they built. The new company was beginning to grow when President Nixon put on an embargo on sales to Russia. This brought wheat prices from $5.00 per bushel down to $3.00, causing sales of the trailer and other products the new company was building, to nothing. The company filed bankruptcy. That was the end of the Farm Pup Trailer. As time passed, farms got

Farm Pup trailers designed by Jon.

larger and semi-tractor trailers replaced smaller trucks.

    I was Sunday school superintendent at First Assembly of God Church in Jamestown. Having held that position for several years, we invited the Sunday school staff out to our farmhouse for a picnic and monthly meeting. As people drove out they commented how nice the fields of waving grain looked. There was a nice crop coming. We had a good meal and the staff left our house at 11:00 p.m. At 12:00 o'clock it started raining and hailing. The hailstorm of 1976 was one of the worst on record. It pounded holes through our garage roof and destroyed one of our three old barns. There were no leaves left on the trees. They were stripped clean with only stub branches left. Later our friends from Nebraska, the George Studlers, our combine customers, remarked about what funny looking trees we grew. Crops were totally gone. Out of 3,000 acres of wheat there were 80 acres worth trying to harvest. Whoa! No harvest meant no crop and no paycheck for one whole year. "Lord," we prayed, "how can we keep up our support to the 15 missionaries we wrote checks to each month and the church and Sunday school support?" Was this Job's test for us? While we had this JES partnership going we tried to keep each enterprise separate to make its own way. Now I was manager of the agriculture department which meant I needed to go look for my own money and survival. Fern and I stood on the Scripture that says,

"And be content with such things as you have;
for he hath said, I will never leave thee, nor
forsake thee" (Hebrews 13:5).

This test was maybe good for Fern and I and the family, but it was tough. During this time we bought old cars. We had to stay home more, budget our eating and special events. We didn't want to fail the people we were supporting.

We had good favor with our banker, Mr. Buegel. We were able to get money enough to keep up with all our missionary pledges and support to the church. We tried to keep a positive attitude and that kept us going. Through all this, God was faithful and we knew:

"All things work together for good, (food,)
to those that love God" (Romans 8:28).

Life wasn't all bad. In 1976 I celebrated my 50th birthday. That year my birthday, July 18th, fell on a Sunday. I took my first real motorcycle ride to church on my birthday. On my way to church I passed Lyle Sjostroms farm. Lyle was mowing grass along the road, so I stopped and had a chat with him. We still talk about my first ride on the cycle. To celebrate, I tried golfing for my first time. Jeff had been learning to fly airplanes the past two years and I began trying a little flying after I was 50. I got my private pilot license in 1978. After Jeff and I got our license, we bought our own Cessna 172, a black and white Sky Hawk. This was a very forgiving airplane. I could fly over farm fields, land on roads, check crops and get back home in a hurry. I remember while farming in South Dakota, 250 miles away, we ran out of sunflower seed while seeding. We threw a few bags of seed into the Sky Hawk and airlifted seed to South Dakota.

With the assistance of Lyle Sjostrom and his expertise we put lights on a runway at the farm with the on/off switch in the house. If I left and didn't get back before dark I could call home and tell them to turn on the runway lights. One time Fern, Jeania and I

Our Cessna 172 airplane

took the laundry to town after dark in the plane.

The year we farmed Tom and Jeannette Waldie's farm, twenty miles away, the plane was real handy. The Waldies had a good grass runway on their farm, which made it handy to check on operations there. One day I flew down to Waldies to check on the combines and tried to land on a gravel road in a strong wind. The air was real squirrelly. I landed on the road and just as I hit ground the plane turned onto an approach and stopped 20 feet from the combine. I am sure I had help from above that time.

The plane was also handy to carry my golf bag. I would land at Waldies' farm and Larry Johnson would pick me up and we would golf at Grand Rapids, N.D. I would fly to Kulm and Lonnie Titus and I would golf nine holes and have lunch, other times we flew to Oakes and golfed with Harvey Wolff.

One day Jon Nitschke called. He couldn't find some cattle. We went up in the plane and spotted them. It was a real windy day with 40 MPH winds when we came back into Jamestown. I asked Jon if he thought we could land in the wind. He wasn't used to flying, he turned white as a sheet.

Two different occasions, in the 172 Cessna, Darryl Justesen accompanied me to different areas of North Dakota to contact farmers about buying some of Concords new grain seeding equipment.

"Sow for yourselves righteousness
reap in mercy, break up your fallow
ground for it is time to see the Lord
till He comes and rains righteousness
on you" (Hosea 10:12).

The year 1977 offered another challenge. Our church sent a group of men to Guatemala to help build a mission church. This was a fun group of people. The group included our leader, Bob Unterseher, Pastor Miller, Jack Wilkenson, Darrel Anderson, Doug Anderson, Reuben, Silas and me, along with men from other churches in N.D. We started by pouring a footing and then laying up cement blocks for walls. Twice a day we would go to what we called the PX, an army term for all kinds of foods and notions. Really it was just a " hole in the wall" store where we could get sodas, ice cream and candy. At least it was a break away from those heavy cement blocks. In two weeks we had the entire roof on, over those blocks of cement. The night before we left, the nationals had their first church service in the building. I had been bitten by some kind of bug, and my hands swelled up like a balloon. The guys said I spent a few delirious nights. I remember the ladies out back making tortillas, standing out under a tree among flies and bugs. That was something else, kind of dried up your appetite.

The reason I mentioned Jack Wilkenson is because we have

Jack Wilkenson and I laying blocks for a church in Guatemala.

become friends also. We have visited their home in Arizona and have been over to their farm for dinners and coffee. For our 50th wedding anniversary they had us over for dinner. Millie fixed a good fried chicken dinner with all the fixin's. When the chicken came around she saw me looking for a special piece. Millie asked, "What are you looking for, Jon?" I said, "A wing." She said, "Oh, I didn't fix the wings." Then with a little small talk about it, we went on with dinner. When we were leaving their house she handed me a paper bag. It had all the wings in it.

I heard Jack tell someone later in years how I had bought some of their farm and he said, "We're still friends." Jack and Millie have since moved off the farm, retiring in one of our rental properties.

Jack and Millie had lost their son, Jim, in a tractor farm accident. Jim and Kathy and Jeff and Sherry were all schoolmates at Montpelier High School. Kathy would come and stay over night with Sherry, she was always fun to have around. Jack and Millie decided to sell off a part of the farm and we were the first one contacted. We bought 320 acres.

"He that knoweth to do good
and doeth it not to him it is sin" (James 4:17).

In 1979 a new opportunity came by. We were offered and bought 1980 acres of the Virgil Rott farm. Why more local farmers did not buy this has always puzzled me, except for the fact that my early army experience (out in the Atlantic) with Jesus, and my walk were working. We had set a goal of giving 30% of our profits to charities by this time.

MIRACLE 18 I'm not sure which of these years it was, when Jeff was bringing in a load of wheat from the Piehl farm, a grasshopper in the cab got too much of his attention and the truck rolled over spilling a full load of wheat into the ditch. He wasn't going fast, luckily he didn't get hurt, there was not much damage on the truck and we got most of the wheat picked up.

Bill and Sherry had been working for Bill's brothers in Minneapolis after they were married. This brings up an interesting story. Bill's brothers had started a tool and die business in the basement of their house. They wanted to upgrade their equipment. Really, they needed a new $5,000 machine to be successful on a bid job. Fern and I loaned them the $5,000 and helped start a business that runs in the millions today. It was encouraging to see them prosper.

When I first started farming I had tried to concentrate on how much I could put into charities and give away and help others. With this I let the Lord provide help on the farm and plug holes of disaster that could arise.

I would like to mention that this time period was the high light of my years of ministry as Sunday School Superintendant. I began in that office in 1965. My first years were under the leadership of our good Pastor Miller. In 1981 the church elected Rev. Jack Glass to be the new pastor. Pastor Glass was an energetic man with lots of ideas, he and myself sitting at Perkins, over a cup of coffee, came up with lots of new plans. It was during his tenure we took the Church and Sunday School Christmas celebration down to the Jamestown Civic Center for the next three years of event there. This was a thrilling accomplishment in my term of office.

"Whoever works his land will have plenty to eat, but the one who chases unrealistic dreams has no sense". (Proverbs 12:11).

/SEVEN/
A NEW PARADIGM OF BUSINESS

Nineteen eighty-two was the beginning of a new era in our harvest combine operations. I feel the Lord saw we were busy enough on the local level and He provided Christian help from here on out. Harvest costs are always a big part of the costs of farming. There is profit in custom harvesting, especially if you can work it around your own crops.

This picture represents 50 years of combining.

With Jeff being home to help, we had rented additional land to where we were farming twice as many acres. Amos Stoltsfus was another one of these guys that once acquainted with us, you never know when they might come back. We met Amos and his wife, Joy, when they were song leaders at a Gerald Derstine Revival in Leeds, North Dakota. Our Dad had met Derstine in Florida under his tent and convinced him to hold meetings in Leeds. That was back in the early 60s. We had become good friends. Here 20 years later Amos called and asked if he could take our combines harvesting to Kansas. Talk about a godsend, Fern and I were tired of the responsibility. Amos and his family operated the harvest for the next five years. Amos was a hustler and really kept things moving. Doors didn't always close on time but he got them closed the next time through.

There are always memories. While working on our crops, we had a two-week rainy spell. About three o'clock one Wednesday afternoon it got dry enough to combine. Wednesday night, being church night, we loaded up for church. I told Amos they could quit and come to church also. He spoke of that event many times and thought it great to be able to quit, after a two-week shut down for rain, and go to church and of course, we have never harvested on Sunday.

"Six days you shall labor and do all
your work, but the seventh day is
the Sabbath to the Lord your God.
On it you shall not do any work" (Exodus 20: 9-10).

MIRACLE 19 Due to the fact that Sherry and Jeffrey had both attended North Central Bible College in Minneapolis, the college people knew where we lived. Their PR man and fundraiser Jack Strom called in 1982. He said apartment units adjacent to the college had come up for sale. They were the Orfield properties, consisting of five buildings, a total of 125 apartments. The Orfields wanted $250,000 down. Colleges don't have a lot of extra money, and being investors we don't keep that kind of money lying around either. We told Jack Strom we thought we could get the money.

It just so happened by this time JES had enough farmland paid off with clear title. We were able to secure money and make the loan to North Central Bible College. Don Argue, president at the time, was very appreciative. President Argue, with his integrity, had us all paid back in five years. About one year after the loan was made, I was asked to serve on the Board of Regents for the college. It has been a good education and fun assignment.

"Doing what is right and fair is more
acceptable to the Lord than offerings of sacrifice"
(Proverbs 21:3).

An opportunity for more farm real estate came in 1983. This land adjoined the Brown farm and was also part of the old Chicago Ranch, known as the Lee farm. Mr. Lee had 470 acres at this location that we wanted and he also had 320 acres that my friend Lyle, wanted. Needless to say, my friend and JES together made an offer and bought it all. Our part was 470 acres.

These friends, Lyle and Evelyn Sjostrom, had become acquainted with us back in the late 60s. Lyle was an employee of Otter Tail Power Co. and when we first met he was living in Holiday Park Village. Lyle bought a farm south of town and started more with cattle. I remember him asking to rent pasture ground. Later he rented some farm ground and we got more involved, then he started buying land. In the mix of all this we were using each other's machinery. Maybe he used more of mine. This is another case where our friendship never ends. In the early years I would do his combining. Lyle would come out after work at Otter Tail, ride with me and drink coffee. He also drove combine and truck for me on kind of a trade-off basis. Sometimes I charged him for work, but we always had fun working together.

One time Lyle and I were harvesting his flax. The flax was bunchy and would plug the combine. Flax is the worst straw to try to pull out of a plugged combine. We tore our nails and laughed and kept going.

Lyle was a good electrician. We were continually putting up buildings for shops and grain-drying equipment. Lyle was always ready to do this work for me. He never once charged for his services.

The offset for us came when he rewired our whole farm base. We had wires hanging from pole to pole, some in bad shape and some broken. Lyle put all our wiring with new wires underground. It included the house, the well, the old shop and the new shop and the grain elevator and drying system. I mean it was first class.

/EIGHT/
FRIENDSHIPS

Leviticus 19:18 says, "Love your neighbor as yourself."

A new part of our business was formed in 1983. Concord Air Seeders was a new concept of farming. The part that makes it air seeding is the fact that behind the seeding tool is a large trailer tank which holds the grain seed and fertilizer. This product is moved from tank to seeder by high volumes of air flowing through tubes taking the metered amount of product with it. The seeder itself could be either a disc drill or shovel-type cultivator. Being new to the industry, there was lots of interest.

Jeff was helping at the farm at the time and helped us remodel our machine storage building into a big heated shop. It was a nice place to assemble equipment. With extra help we were able to set up enough machines to where we were one of the top dealers.

MIRACLE 20 Howard Dahl, president of Concord, made a trip to Florida to see Silas and me for assistance. The plan looked good, we discussed the venture and both decided to go for it. The Concord Company was growing so fast, they were looking for investors. They were looking for high volume help.

Being investors in farms and mobile home parks and now giving 40% of our profits to church and charities, we didn't have piles of money lying around.

I really believe the Lord saw this ahead of time. He had positioned a man in a large Fargo bank who had been a banker in our city, Jamestown, and he knew our character. (One more good connection). We were able to secure the entire funds with just our signature, no collateral. We were able to secure enough money to keep Concord Company going another year.

I believe my Atlantic Ocean experience and my walk to the farm was a big influence for this deal, the best is yet to come.

"And my God will meet all
your needs according to his
glorious riches in Christ Jesus" (Philippians 4:19).

One more fun thing in 1984 was the trip to Portugal when we took our entire family on a MAPS program. We helped on construction of a Bible college complex. Working with cement blocks and cement mud buckets on the second floor was a man-sized job. The cement was pulled up in buckets by rope and pulley. The Duane Henders and the Sam Johnsons were our hosts. Soup and chow furnished by the college was interesting when you found chicken beeks and toes in the soup, but the flavor was always good. Really our accommodations where very good, we had nice clean comfortable beds. This trip I could do again.

Portugal has a lot of interesting history. We toured places such as where Columbus studied his navigation and where he departed to discover America.

I had one of the greatest shocks of my life in October 1985. Jeff and Crystal decided to move to Minneapolis. I had gotten to depend on Jeff to manage things that I wasn't sure I wanted to go back to doing myself. Jeff had such a good handle on equipment changes. New equipment was coming out with monitor controls and computerized applications that I had no knowledge of. You know "I was just born too early and didn't learn all that stuff." I thought this was the end.

We rented out to other farmers all the land we owned and I made plans for an auction sale, which we held in April 1986.

For some reason, I hadn't notified the landlords of 5,000 acres we were renting. I had all winter to think about a plan and decided to keep farming the rented land. Doug Ely and Terry Ost were with us, so we were able to farm. Neighbors said it didn't make sense to rent out our own land and then rent land back from someone else, but it worked.

Terry was an excellent farm helper. He did a lot of maintenance work and trucking in the wintertime. He could even replace truck motors and repair them.

Doug's job was more with seed and chemical sales. We were getting crop chemicals in bulk delivery. Doug would fill farmers' tanks as they came in. We also sold fertilizer and had a mixing machine to make up certain blends.

Now the need had come for more spaces to park homes in Bismarck. Harley Swenson and Harold Schultz had acreage on the east side of town, so we joined together and began construction of Century Park with 530 spaces. This was an easy one with the help of good partners.

"A dream takes on a life of its own."
Robert H. Schuller

/NINE/
GOD'S SOVEREIGN PROTECTION

MIRACLE 21 Later in the fall, Bob came back to the farm one more time to help move some dirt and to maybe earn a few dollars. Things went well until there was an accident. The following is a true story as written up and published in the Pentecostal Evangel, a worldwide magazine published by the Assemblies of God.

Spare His Life God, Spare His Life

I (Bob) set the earth scraper bit in the soil and heard the RPMs of the powerful diesel engine drop as it began to load dirt. Once the bit was set I never looked back. The drainage ditch I was building required precision. Any glance over my shoulder would create a glitch. The 250-horse power tractor bore down as it filled the bucket with rich, heavy soil. I suddenly felt a tremendous impulse to check the loading scraper. I turned my head for a split second and to my horror, I saw the front wheel of the scraper knock a co-worker to the ground. My feet hit the clutch and the brake at the same time. The tractor stopped abruptly. The front wheel of the scraper was sitting directly on top of a man with the scraper half full of dirt.

It was early October. I called Jon Liechty, a businessman and close friend, to ask if he could use some help for a month. He was building a drainage system on one of his farms south of Jamestown, North Dakota. He could use the help so I committed to 30 days. I had operated heavy equipment for Jon in the past, leveling land for mobile home parks.

There were three of us working on the project that day, Wesley Loven, Jon's brother-in-law, and Kenis Loven, Wesley's son. Wesley was our rod man. His job was to read the depth of the cut area to prevent the ditch from going too deep. If too deep the water would stand, if not deep enough it would be a dam.

I lowered the scraper bit to just a couple of inches above the ground as the tractor closed in on the cut area. Wesley, with the eye level, stood with a long stick pointing at the spot where the bit should begin loading the scraper. The bit touched the earth and the tractor began to lug. That's when I looked behind me and saw the front wheel of the scraper hit Wesley and knock him down to the ground. Thousands of pounds of dirt were sitting on top of him.

I grabbed the hydraulic lever to raise the scraper bit. Thoughts were racing through my mind. If I lift the scraper, all the weight of the dirt will crush him for sure. At full throttle I put the tractor in reverse and slowly let out the clutch. Everything was moving in slow motion. Black smoke billowed out of the exhaust pipe as power was transferred to the wheels. The tractor began to jump up and down under the strain, while the scraper bit broke loose from the earth and slowly moved backward. My training as a certified

Emergency Medical Technician, while in a previous pastorate in Colorado, came quickly to mind as I leaped out of the tractor and ran back to where Wesley lay motionless on the ground. The scene was familiar to me. His face was very white indicating a lack of circulation and possible severe internal injuries. He was not breathing and there was no pulse. In my mind, I had just killed my friend.

As I knelt beside Wesley's motionless body, turned my face toward heaven, and in a loud and persistent voice, I cried, "Spare his life, God, spare his life!" I continued to repeat the short prayer until I saw Kenis running from his tractor and scraper to where his father lay on the ground.

"What happened?" he shouted as he ran and fell at his father's side. "I just ran over your dad. Go get the pickup!" I shouted. "Radio the office. Tell the secretary to call the emergency room and tell them that we are on the way!"

I triaged his chest to see if it was crushed. "We will have to do CPR until medical people arrive?," I asked myself. Just then I thought I heard a slight groan. Listening more closely, yes it was! Wesley's eyelids were twitching like he was trying to open them. Listening even closer, I thought, Wesley is trying to tell me something.

Then, more distinctly I faintly heard him say, " Help me up."

Perplexed and with grave concern I shouted, "Wesley, I just ran over you. You probably have internal injuries. Please lay still. We've got to get you to the emergency room."

"Help me up," he emphatically repeated.

By this time Kenis had returned with the pickup. "Your dad wants to stand up." I told Kenis.

I couldn't believe he was alive, let alone talking and wanting to stand up. It didn't occur to me that we had witnessed a miracle.

I looked at Kenis and said, "Okay, help me get him up."

We reached under his arms and lifted him to his feet. He let out a moan and collapsed to the ground. Picking him up again, we quickly put him into the pickup seat and drove out of the field with Wesley pressed hard against the door. We kept glancing at him to see if he was still breathing, it seemed like I heard Wesley say something.

"What did you say?" I asked.

In slow raspy voice he said, "Take me home."

I was sure I hadn't heard right. "Wesley, I just ran over you with the scraper. You may have internal injuries. You could be bleeding inside. You have to go to the hospital." I explained.

In a more stern voice I heard him say, "Take me home."

By this time his wife, Judith had received a phone call about the accident. She was getting ready to go to town when we pulled into the yard. Wesley was sitting up in the truck. Judith came running out of the house and up to the passenger side of the pickup. Wesley rolled the window down and asked her to bring his walker. He explained he was going to take a shower and put on clean clothes.

Judith brought the walker and he slowly made his way into the house without assistance. We were all astonished when he emerged twenty minutes later looking like a new man.

At the hospital a waiting team of medics wondered what was taking us so long. They were waiting outside at the ER entrance with a gurney when we arrived. They quickly rushed him into the examination room. Judith and I waited for over an hour before the doctor appeared asking to see who had run over this man with the scraper. I slowly stood to my feet and raised my hand. The doctor walked promptly to where I stood and asked me to explain what had happened out in the field. I told him every detail I could remember. When I finished he looked puzzled.

The doctor remarked, "I have examined and x-rayed this man for over an hour and I cannot find anything wrong with him. I am going to keep him in the hospital for a few days for observation to make sure everything is alright." This was truly a miracle.

Amos Stoltsfus had run our harvest crew five years and decided he had had enough. He found us a good replacement with John and Pat Swiers. Their family was just getting to the age where he had good built-in help. Pat was also involved very much. I always said she was the best combine operator they had.

Swiers' harvesting crew ran the combines the next thirteen years. Starting in Oklahoma and working their way back to North Dakota each year. They were good with trucks and equipment and still got a lot done. We had real peace of mind when Pat and John were in charge. We knew things were going well and that we would get our fair share.

It was exciting to watch the family children grow up. Each year you would see new expressions on the faces of the four boys. Some of them changed enough in one year we had to ask them their name again. Then there was Jill, their only girl, she was always witty and ready for a laugh.

Driving combines really made an impression on their boys. When their oldest son, Jessie, decided to get married, an outdoor wedding was held. When we got to the wedding, there stood one of our combines. When the wedding service was over at the altar, which was right close to the combine, the bride and groom climbed into the combine and used that as their drive away vehicle. What a blast!!

Four of our John Deere combines operated by John & Pat Swiers' crew.

In 1987 we were offered the opportunity to buy the 96 unit Pheasant Run Apartments in Williston. This was an easy project built along side the airport, good access by airplane. Williston oil drilling was in recession and this let us get a good buy on these units.

This was also the year our Concord Manufacturing Company decided to put an air seeder in the field in Czechoslovakia. Darryl Justesen and I were asked to go. Terry Mortenson, a missionary to that country, was our interpreter. This was behind the Iron Curtain on a 3,000 acre communist farm. The work went well. We had the machine together and running in three days. We ate our meals in their community mess hall. It was interesting to discover that I farmed more acres in North Dakota with three to five hired hands in contrast to their 3,000 acre communist farm that employed five hundred people. Most of their work was done by hand. They made everything from bread and butter to clothes and tools all by themselves. They raised all their own fruits and vegetables and seemed to have a lot of pride in their wineries. There were lots of grapes and huge tanks of wine. They had very modern equipment in the shop.

Eventually it was time to sell our 172 Cessna which I still miss flying today. We bought into a flying group with three other friends who purchased a six passenger Piper Lance with retractable gear. This is a faster plane and carries a bigger load. One day, with the Piper Lance, I flew Darryl Justesen and Jack Oberlander to Kansas to view a new type seed wagon which my friend Ron Neff, and who's father we had combined wheat for many years in the seventies, had developed.

Nineteen eighty-eight was another year of opportunity. The large Freddie Mutschler farm came up for sale. Silas and I bought

Daryl Justeson and I putting a Concord Air Seeder and soil tester in the field in Czechoslovakia.

a total of 2,400 acres giving John Mutschler, a brother of Freddie, an option to buy back 480 acres.

Silas and I had often talked about getting some land in the south to have for our custom harvest run. An ideal number would be a section, 640 acres, of land in each state from North Dakota to Texas.

"Trust in the Lord and do good;
dwell in the land, and feed on his
faithfulness. Delight yourself also in
the Lord and he shall give you the
desires of your heart" (Psalms 37:3-4).

Maybe this was the beginning of our dream. John Mutschler decided to exercise his option. He okayed a trade if we could find land elsewhere. Our friend in Kansas, Adam Nusz, had wanted us to buy land that he could farm in Kansas. Adam had his eye on 480 acres there.

John Mutschler bought those 480 acres and then we traded back with him. That left Silas and I with 1,920 acres of the Mutschler farm. Later Adam Nusz found another 240 acres he wanted to farm nearby in Kansas plus the 480 acres we had traded.

One other sad note this year was the fire of our farm shop. It being December and winter time we had the 120 X 60 building full of equipment. A new John Deere combine, three tandem grain trucks, two tractors, a Concord Air Seeder, antique Ford tractor, and thousands of dollars of tools all burned up plus the building burned to the ground. Often we wonder why, but never underestimate God's plan.

In January of 1990 Fern and I went on another MAPS trip to Argentina with a church group from Eden Prairie, Minnesota. Fern helped make bed furniture for the dorms. I laid up cement blocks on a three-story college building. These are great times of refreshing, using your talents to help build something for other people, people that have nothing to build with and nowhere to get it. We both thank the LORD for one more opportunity to give back some things we have been blessed with. Rocky and Sherry Grams, Mike and Mona Shields were our hosts.

The year of 1990 was both a good year and a sad year. This was the year the mother of us boys passed away. Mom had lived a full life of 96 years. According to my estimation she was one of the great ladies of all time. There wasn't a selfish bone in her body. Mom was always helping someone. At the age of 90, she was still going to the nursing homes, singing and playing the piano for the older residents there. Her grandchildren spent a lot of Saturday noons with her for lunch. Mom could make, it seemed like, lots of food out of nothing and it was really good. Fried cornmeal mush, baked beans, potato salad, and homemade bread were some of her specialties. Dandelion salad with hard-boiled eggs was another. She made homemade cheese and green peppers filled with sauerkraut.

The most outstanding part of her life was her prayer time. You could count on each day after noon lunch, Mom would go to some corner of the house and pray. We never heard what she said but you can be sure she named all her children and grandchildren many times.

I count it a modern day miracle, when divorce rates are 50%, none of her six children and only two out of twenty-two of her grandchildren ever went through a divorce.

"She keeps a close eye on the conduct of her family,
and she does not eat the bread of idleness. Her children
and her husband stand up and bless her. Many women

have done a noble work, but you have surpassed them all."(Proverbs 31:27-29)

Another farm, the 960 acre Hoggarth farm, came up for sale. This was our first irrigated ground. The farm had two pivots on it. There was plenty of water below. We tried potatoes one year on our own, but we didn't have proper contracts so we went back to cash rent. As of now, we have a man cash renting the ground for potatoes every 2nd or3rd year. I have been farming the ground in the years in between.

The 90s brought us into a new goal of giving with all we had going. We thought we should try to give 50% of our profits away. I can't tell you how it works, except we know Jesus helped us many times. Sometimes we had normal setbacks, but it was our test and with determination we always came out on top.

"Give and it will be given to you. A good measure, pressed down, shaken together and running over, will be poured into your lap. For with the measure you use, it will be measured to you" (Luke 6:38).

MIRACLE 22 Before we get moved away from the Montpelier farm I should tell you about our neighbor, Frank. Frank moved in on a section of land right next to our farm. He was a very reserved type of fellow. I watched him farm several years right across the road. Driving past him on a tractor he never would wave or recognize that he ever saw you. I thought the guy must be mad at me. One day I got my tractor stuck across the fence from him. I thought, "This may be my chance to try him out." I walked over and asked if he would pull me out. "Yes," he said. He gave me a pull, wouldn't take any money for it, and this was the beginning of our friendship. We got to be good friends. Frank started coming over to our place to talk farming. Being I was farming more than he, he ask me how I could sleep at night and how I knew where to start each day. In a few years Frank got sick with cancer and ended up in the hospital. I visited him a few times, prayed with him, and led him to the Lord before he died. I was asked to be one of his pallbearers at his funeral.

/TEN/
NEW OPPORTUNITIES FOR BUSINESS AND MINISTRIES

As I stated before in chapter four, two men I have observed for years, I find an interesting and maybe a sad conclusion. Jim and Joe were cousins. Jim you might say was born with a silver spoon in his mouth. Joe on the other hand came from a poor home. His father was an alcoholic. Jim started farming the home place where his dad left off. Joe got started farming by renting a small piece of ground.

Sorry to say Jim died fairly early after middle age. He had lost some of the farm that was handed over to him. Many times I saw Jim go through our little town and stop for a beer which cost him both time and money.

Joe accumulated much farm land and has great holdings of property. The lesson here is, it's not how much you start with, as much, as how you manage what you have. It isn't always good to start a man with money, when he doesn't know where it came from or how it got there.

There were two other tycoon farmers who were interesting to watch, and when I thought I was in a slow pace, trying to hang on, it seemed there was nothing that could stop Bill and Ben. I took a farm tour out to Bills large tractor barn with six big John Deere tractors and equipment. Bens farm with ten tractors, airplanes, and motor homes, don't know what really happened, these guys just couldn't hang on to all their property and investments. You would have thought they were on top of the world financially.

The nineteen eighties were stressful dry years. Anyone who was overleveraged at the bank had tough going. Slowly Bill and

Ben started selling off their properties, some was foreclosed on until Ben had nothing left and Bill had very little. Sad to say none of these guys ever took time for church and probably never gave much to charities. The Lord wants at least 10% or more.

New doors opened in 1991 to buy the 96 Carriage House apartments in South Dakota. There were 24 very deluxe units in four different cities, although some units needed some work, they seem to stay full all the time.

A new association had begun in 1991 with Todd Sjostrom, our friends Lyle and Evelyn's son. Todd came as a helper in the harvest field. He drove combines and trucks. As a college student he was very sharp, yet very polite and easy to work with. Todd had one accident like anyone could have, he rolled over a truckload of wheat on Highway 46. It wasn't speed as much as a top heavy load and there was not much damage on the truck. The wheat was easy to pick up as most of it fell on the black top road. All it took was a grain auger and scoop shovels to clean it up.

MIRACLE 23 This story goes on and on, actually started by taking a neighbor girl, Marilyn Johnson, to Sunday school, written up earlier in this book. We soon turned north up towards Yakima. This was the place where Marilyn and Tim Waddington were living. Actually Tim grew up in this area. Remember, Marilyn was our little Sunday school girl. Tim wanted to show me 80 acres of pasture he wanted to rent to make hay and run a few cows. I went back and talked to Silas and we offered him a 50-50-share crop deal.

This was just the beginning. The next year Tim found 320 acres we could rent and now we needed 50 cows. This new acreage was alfalfa hay ground. We could irrigate the ground and sell hay to the dairies. This seemed to work well and made jobs for Tim's children who were in their mid-teens. Tim kept going and finding more hay ground for rent. Tim had pushed up acreage to 600 acres and some extra pasture, which needed 150 cows. We were still working on our 50-50-share crop deal. Watch for more of the Waddington miracle chapters ahead.

Back home, some of Bob Reimer's land came up for sale in 1992. This was right beside the Hoggarth farm and seemed like it fit into our mix. We purchased 860 acres.

We bought a small acreage right by the Erickson farm, 250 acres, in 1993. It was so close it connected right in.

This same year we took another MAPS trip to Homestead, Florida. Hurricane Andrew had destroyed a lot of the city, partly taking down the Assembly of God Church and parsonage. We were with a group that included Bob Unterseher (our group leader), Keith Veil, Joe Beckstrand, Jeannie and Gary Anderson. Also on the job we made new friends with Norvel and Arlene Johnson from York, North Dakota. Fern and Jeannie cooked for the group of workers. We ate good with cooks like that, just one more chance to work for Jesus.

At the end of this same year, Bob Unterseher took us with a group of workers to the Canary Islands where Bruce and Bonita Thomas were the missionaries. This was one of the better MAPS trips we had. The Islands were beautiful, many, many flowers and we found whole sides of hills that had blossomed out with pretty colors. All the colors you can imagine were on sides of buildings and street signs and light poles. The housing where we stayed was several miles from our work site. They needed someone to drive, who could drive an older stick shift vehicle with steering wheel on the right side. I took the test. The missionaries said they were impressed and I got the job. It was a new experience driving on the left side of the road, especially meeting traffic. My days were filled driving all over the island getting groceries and supplies for 20 some workers. On our return trip we made a stop in Madrid, Spain. Bob had told our Madrid host that people were getting low on cash, so he should get a low priced hotel. The place he picked was on such a narrow street the bus couldn't drive there. We had to carry our luggage one and one half blocks.

MIRACLE 24 I was entering the hotel that night, on a dark side of the street, two young guys tried to rob me. One came in front, poking fingers in my face while the other guy tried to get my back pockets. I had often thought if I got in trouble I would try to holler real loud to get attention for help. So I did. The guy in back grabbed my left pocket tearing that pocket out and the side seam of my pants, way down to the cuff at the bottom. Bob heard me and saw the young guy, so he grabbed him by the throat and tried to choke him. The young guys broke loose by hitting Bob in the chest with his fist and ran out the door. My credit cards fell out on the floor but the robbers didn't get anything. PTL! We were thankful they didn't have any weapons!

There was very little sleep that night. The staircases were narrow and lighting was poor. People were moving desks and refrigerators in front of the doors of their rooms for fear of break-ins. There was noise on the streets all night long.

No weapon formed against you shall prosper!
(Isaiah 54:17).

Beautiful springtime came in March 1995and we were on our way to Russia and the U-kraine along with a group of Concord's air seeder customers. Among the group going with us were Howard and Ann Dahl, Jerry and Arvilla Peerboom, Ron and Rita St. Croix with their daughter Renee, and several others.

Visiting in the Ukraine we toured a few different farms to look at their styles of farming and the type of equipment they were using and explain the Concord air seeding system.

Among one of these farms we were invited in for a noon meal. The meal was served on a long table that would seat twenty to twenty five people. There was no heat in the building, the temperature out side being about 40 degrees, snow on the ground, it was cold inside at the table. They tried doing their best to keep the food warm but that was hard. They seemed to enjoy lots of Vodka and maybe that kept them warm inside warming up their spirits.

Our ride on a Russian train back to St. Petersburg was a neat experience. We spent two night in sleepers on the train paired up with two couples in each small room. Small beds and no place to hang clothes, bathroom down the hall for the night trips, it got real interesting. We were fortunate enough to pair up with the Peerbooms in our room, they were good sleepers and every one ignored the snoring. At St. Petersburg we boarded planes back to the US.

In 1995 Tim Waddington had found a farm for sale in Yakima Valley. It was 170 acres of irrigated hay, plus another 120 acres of Indian ground we could rent. This was the Harry Kwak farm, increasing Tim's acreage up near 900 acres.

It was in the middle 90s when another opportunity opened up in Chicago. A nephew of Silas and Martha, Glenn Mueller, and also son of the late Carl Mueller, wanted financial help on construction of rental buildings. Needless to say this has grown to larger dimensions than was ever thought. Remodeling up to 60 unit apartments and condo buildings. Glenn has done a great job on this and is still continuing to grow. We have had good returns

Sitting on a 4 x 4 x 8 alfalfa bale weighing one ton at Yakima Valley farm.

Cutting cattle by horse on Yakima ranch

on our investments.

MIRACLE 25 In 1995 we had a big year at Concord Air Seeders. You remember back in 1985 when Silas and I had arranged money for Concord, some of which we later took in stock. At this time, both John Deere and Case IH wanted to buy our Air Seeder Company. Through Howard Dahl, president of the company, and his good sense of negotiating, the price kept going up. We wound up getting 10 times our investment of stock.

"Honor the Lord with your wealth, with
the firstfruits of all your crops; then
your barns will be filled to overflowing,
and your vats will brim over with new
wine" (Proverbs 3:9-10).

I feel the Lord gave me new insight for farming in 1991. As I wrote before, after Jeff left, and Fern and I moved to town, we rented out the land we owned and I kept farming the rented land. We decided to share crop the rented land. We paid more of the cash outlay, my farmer share croper provided more of the work. We divided seed and fertilizer costs, each of us taking one-half of the crop. This new arrangement let me sell some of our equipment we didn't need. We had a good auction sale, sold some equipment but not the combines and trucks we used in the harvest. We could do some of the harvesting of our crops and also do custom combining, which we have done all our lives. This was our third farm machinery auction.

MIRACLE 26 I must say, during the last five years, with Jeff being gone, the Lord provided the farm with the best of help. It is a blessing to look back and see how He put each one in our path such as Wesley, Henry, Doug, Terry, Fred, Bob, Amos, John, Gerrit, Lyle, Todd, Arthur, John Swiers and others. I appreciated each one of them and with the help of the Lord I can say:

"My help comes from the Lord,

the maker of heaven and earth" (Psalms 121:2).

On this last page I mentioned our park at Dundee, Florida. Back in 1976, Jon and Silas purchased Dell Lake Village. The park had a clubhouse close to Dell Lake. The park was built to accommodate 250 mobile homes. This was a slow time in Florida. A bank had repossessed the park. There were only 15 homes in place. We thought we had made a fair deal on the park and bought it. It took five years to fill up the spaces. After that, things went along fairly smoothly. Silas and I and our wives each had a home in the park. Fern and I stayed there until the winter of 2007.

MIRACLE 27 The park in Florida had been an enjoyment in our lives. When we sold the park we put 10% of the money it sold for into the "Donor advised fund with the Assemblies of God Foundation." Each year Silas and I direct income off the funds to many different ministries.

"The only joy of living is the joy of giving."

-Robert Schuller

Remember I wrote about our good friends Howard and Ann Dahl? Here we are together again. Howard is president of the balance of our Concord company we kept which is now named Amity. Howard and Ann Dahl asked Fern and me to go to Dallas, Texas, to be a guest at a Luis Palau President's Conference. This was a real eye-opener as to the size of his evangelism. To be able to meet such a humble man, one who talks to everybody, and to meet some of the great financial men of the country was a wonderful thing. We met David Hall, owner of the Phoenix Suns, Fred Sewell, owner of a large gas and oil company, Norman Miller, the owner of the Interstate Battery company, Jay Bennett a lawyer with large real estate holdings in Minneapolis, Howard Dahl, manufacturer of sugar beet equipment with sales in Europe and Russia; Wayne Huizenga, with large holdings all over Florida; Dan Konell, national football player, Sean Stepeltong, famous ball player and Stephen Tchividjian, nephew of Billy Graham. These are the kind of people supporting Luis Palau.

We had the privilege in 1996 of financially helping a lady. Her husband left her with three school age children. Debbie was a good mother who worked hard. She always had a job but that didn't cover the expense of bringing up a family. She also fell behind on some medical bills. We gave her enough to buy their groceries for over one year, and have helped periodically since.

"He that knoweth to do good and doeth it

not, to him it is sin" (James 4:17).

MIRACLE 28 In 1997 Tim Waddington was calling again, another 150 acre farm came up for sale. This place had two extra mobile homes for housing. He needed a place for his growing

Marilyn and Tim Waddington 25th Wedding Anniversary

family to live. There was also a large shop building he could use for repairing and storing equipment. The farm was all seeded down to alfalfa hay, a perfect fit for what we were doing there.

This put the Waddington's operation, along with more rented land, up to over 1,200 acres of irrigated hay, corn and wheat. Also the cow herd had been increasing to 300 or more and now the final total of cows is 500 head.

This is the type of miracle that has developed just by taking a little young girl to Sunday school. What the Lord started 30 years ago, He planned it right. We have been sharecropping, reaping the benefit all this time.

Tim never forgot his calling to serve the Lord. He does a lot of weekend ministry and singing. They are a great Christian family, along with us, believes what Jesus said:

"Seek first the kingdom of God and His

righteousness, and all these things

shall be added unto you" (Matthew 6:23).

Later we got to take an interesting trip to Hong Kong with Luis Palau in 1997. Luis went over for a citywide crusade just ahead of the time when Hong Kong would fall back into the hands of China.

Hong Kong had been under the control of the British until this time. We were asked to go along as prayer partners and help distribute advertising in the city. This was a very modern, busy place. Most all of the American vendors were there, everything from Kentucky Fried Chicken to McDonalds hamburgers. There were also very nice American clothing stores.

Luis held the crusade in a large 40,000-seat arena, which had a roof that could be opened or closed. Large crowds attended and completely filled the arena on the last Sunday. Many decisions for

Christ were made.

"The Lord is my light and my salvation
Whom shall I fear?
The Lord is the stronghold of my life
of whom shall I be afraid?" (Psalm 27:1).

From Hong Kong, Fern and I left the party and flew to Tokyo, Japan. A missionary couple met us at the airport and escorted us for three days. We had never seen so many people in all of our lives. We rode the city transit systems, every stop just jammed full of people, both men and women in black apparel. Ladies wore black skirts, white blouses with small black ties and the men wore white shirts, black ties and black coats. With their black hair it was a beautiful sight. We stood on the trains looking down at several hundred people going to work and never have I seen anything more matched looking. It was like seeing a flock of sheep. They all looked alike.

I must say it was hard to find food that we liked. Had it not been for our missionary friend we would have been in big trouble. A lot of their diet comes from the sea. They fix it so differently and some was eaten raw. Our systems couldn't digest it.

The scenery was great. We didn't realize Japan was quite mountainous. Because land is very scarce, the Japanese don't waste one square inch of ground. Either the earth is covered with buildings and streets, or is growing usable vegetation, hillsides and all. The country as a whole was very clean.

"When I consider your heavens, the work of Your
fingers, the moon and the stars, which You have
ordained, what is man that You are mindful of him.
You have made him to have dominion over the
works of Your hands. How excellent is Your

name in all the earth!" (Psalms 8:3-9)

MIRACLE 29 Earlier I told you about Todd Sjostrom and me selling seed and working together. In 1997 Pioneer decided to make computers a mandatory part of seed sales. I was born too early, didn't grow up with computers and this really spooked me out of business.

"Don't give up on the brink of a miracle.

God's power makes His possibilities achievable!"

-Robert Schuller

This is exactly what happened. Todd had been selling for me on a commission basis. Pioneer agreed to let us do a flip-flop. Todd would be the dealer and I could sell under him. This was an absolute miracle. Normally I would have had to quit business. This was just at the turning point of soybean farming coming into our area. No one would have dreamed how large the soybean sales would become.

At my age, 71, this was an easier way for me. I just needed to book orders and Todd had all the responsibility with Pioneer. The size of sales grew from soybean sales to where I am making three to four times as much money now as before. I would have missed this miracle without it.

/ELEVEN/
NEW LEADERSHIP

MIRACLE 30 Nineteen ninety-eight was also the beginning of a new thrust in our family operation. Jeff called one day, after being on his own for 15 years, and asked if he could join our operation. It was the right timing for Dad. I was now in my 70's, wanting to give up some responsibilities. What do you know, we got our son back home! I was one happy father waiting several years for this to happen.

Super corn crop on New Mexico irrigated farm.

"For the eyes of the Lord go back and forth
throughout the land to strengthen those
whose hearts are fully committed to Him!"
(2 Chronicles 16:9).

Now with Jeff back working with us, we began to look for expansion in various areas. Like I said before, I was looking for farms from North Dakota to Texas.

In the High Plains Journal, a farm was advertised in New Mexico, just three miles from the Texas border. I wondered if this was my Texas answer. With Jeff living in Dallas, he could go check it out. He did all the legwork. Being a pilot, Jeff could look at different farms in short order. He drew up working agreements with the seller and found a good renter to farm the ground. After Jeff had everything in place, Silas and I went down for the closing. This was an 800 acre irrigated farm with 5 pivets on it.

From here on out Jeff had pretty much control of dealing with renting out our own properties. There are a total of 15 different farmland renters to deal with.

Like I said, I continued renting other people's land and farming that, some of it on a share crop basis. When dealing with share croppers, there are right and wrong decisions to make. Sometimes it may seem that two different ways are both right. I was working out a crop insurance report and wondering whose answer was right. That very night as I turned to Proverbs for devotional reading I got my answer and made my decision.

"Dishonest scales are disgusting to the Lord,
but accurate weights are his delight" (Proverbs 11:1).

MIRACLE 31 In 1999 a new opportunity opened up for us for manufactured home sales in another city. One hundred forty acres up against the south side of Minot was offered to us. It was still considered farmland and was bought for that kind of price.

The next year, after buying the land at Minot, we put in a sales office and began construction of Prairie Bluff for manufactured housing, which included building 169 spaces. We already have large corporations wanting to buy part of this property.

"God doesn't say "No." He does say "Grow!"
-Robert Schuller

He that soweth sparingly shall also reap sparingly,
He that soweth bountifully shall also reap
Bountifully,
Every man according as he purposeth in his heart,
so let him give;
Not grudgingly, or of necessity: for God loveth
a cheerful giver.   (2 Corinthians 9: 6-7).

By this time, John Swiers' family was all grown into adulthood. Jessie and Justin were both married and had children of their own. They just couldn't make the combine run down south. Then the best driver and stabilizer, Pat, underwent back surgery.

It was time to reduce the harvest fleet from four units down to two. Jon and Silas had a farm equipment auction sale a FOURTH time. We sold off two combines, extra trucks, trailers and miscellaneous equipment. This was a successful sale.

MIRACLE 32 Our next farming attempt was in Minnesota. We purchased 970 acres with six irrigation pivots on it. There being a lot of water, it looked like a good farm to buy. We were able to pick up some added blessings on this farm. Normally on irrigation pivots there are corners on every field that don't get water, which leaves those areas as non-profitable. We were able to get a CRP contract on the corners making a payment each year. Also another offer came from a Minneapolis firm wanting to put up wind towers to generate electricity. We have had three towers put up with hope of getting three more. The income from those two plums will pay more than half the interest costs on the farm.

MIRACLE 33 Back to our drive in Bismarck, Dave was showing me some possible sights where they might build a church. The property they were looking at was way out in the far edge of town with no good accessibility. I drove him by a new piece of property we had acquired for placing manufactured housing. Our two parks, one of 400 spaces and the other of 530 spaces, were almost full, so we needed to look for more land. We bought 40 acres on the north side along a busy main road into Bismarck. One corner along the road was zoned commercial and would make a good spot in a residential area for the new church.

That was exactly what happened. Connie's Dad, Gordon Nickell, who had moved to Bismarck, was an architect and had drawn many church plans.

It's thrilling to see how the Lord can put things together, like Pastor Dave, architect Gordon and us as property owners.

Now stands the new large Capital Christian church facility that will include an educational department. Dave says the Lord had us buy that property just so he could build His church. He also moved Gordon to Bismarck just for that reason.

Our blessing was the fact that we got some tax relief for the gift.

"The mind of man plans his ways.

But the Lord directs his steps!" (Proverbs 16:9).

Capital Christian Center, Bismark

/ TWELVE /
GOD'S HEALING TOUCH

In April of 2001, I brought shocking news to everyone. We had just returned home from Florida. It was my first day out to the farm. I was repairing a truck tarp and up on a ladder stretching over the side as far as possible. I got a pain in my right arm. I knew it wasn't an ordinary pain.

Having some loose parts to take to town for repair, I took them in to Midwestern Machine, owned by my friend, Keith Veil, to get fixed up and the pain in my arm continued to grow. I had planned to stop in town for lunch. By this time I was really hurting and decided to head for home.

I called Fern and said I'd be home for lunch. Fern had lunch ready. I ate and said I would sit down and rest. I had no sooner sat down when the pain started traveling up my neck. I called Fern, "Get me to the emergency room as soon as possible!"

I didn't know why she needed to change clothes. Why didn't she drive faster? "Don't stop at that stop sign. Let's go!" I was in desperate pain.

As soon as I arrived, they had me lie down, clothes and all and put nitroglycerin tablets under my tongue. This definitely cut down the pain. After Dr. Johnson's diagnosis, he said, "you were trying to have a heart attack." I responded, "I'm not trying very hard." Dr. Johnson said I definitely had heart blockage. They placed me in an ambulance and took me to Bismarck Med Center One Hospital.

I arrived on Friday evening. Since the doctors were gone for the weekend, they just kept me in bed and stabilized me until Monday when they ran tests. Wednesday, April 25 2001, they prepared me for open-heart surgery.

About now is when I began to have sobering thoughts, especially when the doctor came in and had me sign a paper releasing him from liability in case I died. I must say that in and through these thoughts I had perfect peace. Some people say they think of things they wish they had done. Well, I didn't have any of this. My slate must have been clear. Thank the Lord.

By this time, our daughters Sherry and Jeania had both flown in to be with Mom during the surgery. The nurses were terrific. They must have given me something to put me out. I don't even remember leaving the room on the way to surgery.

The doctor would come out periodically and tell Mom and the girls how I was doing, like, "we've got his heart out," "he is running on a machine," and "doing fine," "now we've put his heart back in and it started." I guess the worst thing for them was when they saw me come out of surgery, all the tubes hooked up all over, three in my stomach, two down my throat and one in my nose. They tell me this is when Mom and the girls lost it.

I came out of the four-by-pass surgery just fine. The nurses started walking me the second day. I was doing so well that in three days I could take my own shower.

My recovery went real well. Looking back, except for the healing power of Jesus—"By His stripes we are healed," it could have been like this inscription I read on a tombstone.

"I used to be where you are
Soon you will be where I am
Are you prepared to join me?"
    In recovery these words came to me:
      We came down life's road
      On kind of an easy way.

Each day gathering a heavier load
Thinking forever we would stay.

All of a sudden
On an ordinary day,
Life faltered, it halted
In an unusual way.

Pain persisted to twist my arm
And up my neck it did ride.
I knew someone had set the alarm
To the doctor I went—Fern as my guide.

This summer will end
The third quarter of life's game.
(on this side of death)
We'll play the fourth quarter

Holding on to Jesus' name.
Thankful for the second chance,
So when He calls again
We will know we won the game.
We know that Jesus will
Add to life its length.
Psalm 118:14 says "He is my strength."

/THIRTEEN/
ADDITIONAL CONNECTIONS

Fern and I thanked the Lord that after surgery recovery, 2002 went on pretty normal. We were back to taking trips. We were able to go to Seattle for a Luis Palau festival. There were huge crowds of up to 100,000 people. Having been to several of the Palau President's conferences we were able to go into the VIP tent. That is where the heart of the whole festival is located. You meet some of the greatest people in the world.

The year 2002 was just busier than ever. This was a year when money didn't seem to stop long enough to know we had the stuff around. We had finally reached a new plateau in our charitable contributions. Now we were supporting 50 different people on a monthly basis, places including missionaries, colleges, and our local church and civic affairs, giving up to and sometimes over 50% of our profits.

"Bring ye all the tithes into the storehouse,
that there may be meat in my house, and
prove me now herewith, saith the Lord of
hosts, if I will not open the windows of
heaven, and pour you out a blessing that
there shall not be room to receive it. And I
will rebuke the devourer for your sakes and he
shall not destroy the fruits of your ground
                              (Malachi 3:10-11).

"Always look at what you have left.
Never look at what you have lost."

The year 2003 opened avenues to put our money where our mouth is. There were several hurting people that needed help to get over a hurdle.

"Jesus himself said, "It is more blessed
to give than to receive." (Acts 20:35)

We had the opportunity of making five digit loans to the following people.

A construction company friend.

A main street business man.

A friend with a surgical operation.

A friend with church construction.

A friend with huge medical problems.

These were all with no security, and no interest was charged.

This was also the year a young farmer came to us for help. This man became liable for a half million dollars for which he was not at fault. The courts gave him a bad rap. Because of this, the man lost his credibility at local banks. We put up loans to help him, giving him money enough to farm for the next two years.

"He that knoweth to do good
and doeth it not to him it is sin"

(James 4:17).

Howard and Ann Dahl and the Amity Company hosted our second trip. This was an agricultural trip to Moscow, Russia. Amity is the leading manufacturer of sugar beet machines working around the Black Sea area. We went to see them work as well as make new contacts for more sales. We were on farms as large as 25,000 acres. One of these farms had 25 Amity sugar beet lifting machines. Some of these farms owned their own sugar factories. With cheap labor they made sugar very competitive for the U.S. We saw huge piles of raw sugar beets rotting away, all moldy and smelly, waiting to be processed into sugar.

It was time to buy another farm in Texas, 635 irrigated acres in one section, complete with four pivots, wells, pumps and motors. This farm was just put together three years prior to our purchase and had good modern equipment on it. Another good feature was the fact that Harold Meyers, our farmer in New Mexico, wanted to farm this place also. Harold is a super individual, a good farmer and always pays on time. This was another one of those great connections the Lord put in our life.

Now it was time again for the Homes division to expand in manufactured home sales. A sales company in Rapid City, South Dakota and Gillette, Wyoming wanted to sell out. Curt, Bob and Kent negotiated a deal that looked reasonable. This gave us five retail outlets in three states.

"Thus far has the Lord helped us" (1 Samuel 7:12).

"It is no secret what God can do.
What he's done for others, he will
do for you."

At the North Central University partners banquet they presented me a plaque and gift for 20 years of service and let me address the crowd of 500 people. What a challenge! Our friend Mike Shields was banquet speaker. Getting ahead of Mike on the program was a first for me. We worked with him on a Bible College in Argentina, where he always beat me to the chow line. It was a thrill to be able to present Dr. Gordon Anderson a check from the Liechty family to the University for $50,000. This was another banner year in our efforts of giving.

"Let us not grow weary in well doing
For at the proper time
We shall reap a harvest

If we do not give up" (Galatians 6:9).

If there is anything I would like to stress, it would be that everyone needs that walk where it is just you and Jesus, and you can talk to Him.

"Jesus said, Ask and it will be given
you; seek and you will find; knock
and the door will be opened to you" (Luke 11: 9).

Our first major trip in January 2005 was with Priority One directed by Joyce and Sam Johnson. Sam is a friend who grew up with us in North Dakota. The five day cruise took us to Cozumel, Mexico. Along with us were Silas and Martha Liechty, Norvel and Arlene Johnson from York, North Dakota. Dan, Sam's brother, was on this cruise also. Dan gave me some good ideas about writing books. He encouraged me to get going on this book.

The purpose of the cruise was to raise money to build Bible Schools in Romania and Russia. We were glad we could be a part of another worthy cause and donate funds to this cause.

The Luis Palau President's conference and the Book of Hope rally were both held in February on the east coast of Florida. What great refreshing messages, reports of thousands turning their lives over to Jesus. What fellowship with the greatest people on earth. The reports were so inspiring we just couldn't help but dig deep and give donations to each of these ministries.

Leaving Florida heading for Texas our main objective in Houston was to find the church of Joel Osteen. We had an address, and finding it before dark, a lady at the parking lot said Joel would be speaking that Saturday night. We stayed and enjoyed the service. People came from everywhere. Some walked, some had old beat up cars and some cars were newer. Although it was Saturday night, the 4000 seat auditorium was full. After the service Joel invited all visitors to join him behind the platform. It was nice to talk to him, shake his hand and also take a picture with Joel.

On Memorial Day weekend 2005, the mayor of Jamestown, Charles Kourajian, at our church, presented Jim Gackle, Daboldt Ketterling and myself each a high school diploma. The North Dakota legislature gave high school diplomas to all World War II veterans who entered Army service before graduating from high school. I really felt honored to have this diploma. Only problem now, people told me maybe I could go get a real job.

Soon after seeding time, Kevin Hollar, my friend and irrigation equipment specialist, and I made a fast trip to Kimball to look at the farm we missed coming home earlier. We made a cash offer on the farm, but by this time the farmer decided not to sell. I still know the Lord has something for us in Nebraska. I awakened one night in a somber mode thinking about my calling and a deep sense of responsibility came over me. I went into tears realizing I needed help. I cried out, "Jesus, Jesus help me, Jesus help me." I wept myself to sleep. In the morning I felt the load was lifted. It was like a fresh new start; I was back on track again.

As I wrote before, I never worried about obtaining hired help. That was the Lord's part to arrange, if we were to continue supporting missionaries, churches, colleges, evangelists, and other charities. I can recall many people would come just at the right time to fill a position on the farm. Following is a list of people the Lord had provided through a period of 50 years.

June Were	Jim Gackle
Allen Martin	Allen Fercho
Amos Stultsfus	Adam Nusz
Adam Liechty	Art Duncklee
Bob Bachman	Bob Unterseher

Bill Owen	Cris Paulsen
Curtis Liechty	Darwin Verke
David Sjostrom	Doug Meyer
Doug Ely	Dan Rueb
Darryl Wileman	Earl Loken
Edwin Nitschke	Earl Fercho
Fred Hoffman	Gene Wolf
Gerrit Van Bruggen	Henry Rasmussen
Harvey Wolff	Harvey Loven
Jamie Beechy	Jeff Liechty
Jeff Glass	John Swiers
Kenis Loven	Larry Nitschke
Lester Peterson	Llewelyn Paulsen
Lyle Vilhauer	Merlin Trapp
Terry Ost	Paul Liechty
Todd Sjostrom	Walter Bartel
Wayne Rolle	Wesley Loven
Harold Odegard	Cris Paulsen
Mick Hessler	

MIRACLE 34 Now we needed help on our Minnesota farm and through the providence of God a Pennsylvania Dutchman, another Mennonite family, Allen and Bertha Martin and their eight children came driving through North Dakota looking for work. They drove west on I-94 to Dickinson, North Dakota, 200 miles beyond Jamestown, our place of business. After spending two days there, they turned around and drove back to Jamestown. Looking for a place to stay overnight they went to the Star Motel. This motel was owned by Christian people, Dick and Jean Seekins, who attended the same church we attended. Mr. Seekins brought the Martin family along to church and introduced me to Allen who

Seeding on the Minnesota farm.

said he was looking for work.

Allen and I discussed several places he had been to and the kind of work he had done. I called three references he gave, all saying good things about Allen. On Tuesday we hired Allen.

Allen fit well in the farm program. We were able to rent a new quad-track Case-IH tractor, and a new no-till air seeder, to seed the Minnesota farm. This was the most modern, electrical over hydraulic, computerized, equipment available. Allen crawled on the machine and basically never stopped until the job was done.

You probably wonder where his wife and eight children hung out. We

Martin children, harvesting the Minnesota farm.

gave them residence in a mobile home in our Holiday Park Village. Although that was home, Bertha would load up the children in their custom built van along with a tent and cooking supplies and park out in the same field Allen was working in. It was fun to see the children play and run after birds and rabbits in the warm sandy soil. Bertha was able to cook up some real good meals out in the field that even I got to enjoy.

Was Allen a God-send? I know in my heart he was. Things like this don't just happen. Someone was looking out for us. PTL!

Jesus referred to needy people as having them with us always. It was our pleasure to help one of our Christian family friends, a family with three children, get out of credit card debt by setting up the debt on a three- year repayment plan to us. No interest charged here.

One day walking into our local grocery store I saw a friend checking out a full cart of groceries. Something inside me said, go pay for his food bill. I told my friend, "it's my turn to pay." When I got the bill it was over 200 dollars. The man needed help. He was feeding the children by himself, the mother had left them, leaving them to shift alone.

Another person called from out of town asking if we would deposit money in his bank account. We were glad to help. He had written too many checks and was overdrawn at the bank. The ironic part of this is that this same man a few years ago tried to shut down my farming operation. He wrote a letter to my landlord and to me stating that he wanted the land away from me. He stated in his letter "it is time for the Jon Liechty empire to come down."

"Jesus said,

Love your enemies;

do good to them that hate you

and pray for them that
despitefully use you."

(Matthew 5:44).

One more time Kevin Hollar and I got into our 150 Ford truck and headed south through Nebraska, Colorado, Oklahoma, and Kansas looking for one more farm. To reach my original goal, we have Nebraska and Oklahoma yet to pursue. Kevin is a good driver and has a good eye for irrigation farms. All I needed to do was to enjoy the scenery.

We are right at the end of year 2005. As of this writing we have made offers on two Nebraska farms. Hoping something will come together. I knew the Lord had a farm for me in Nebraska. At the end of this writing we were able to purchase 320 acres of irrigated ground in Nebraska in 2006. Kevin and I did take a serious look at an irrigation farm in Oklahoma, I tried negotiating a price, but that is yet to come.

"See it is to believe it; believe it is to see it."

Joel Osteen

I wrote earlier in chapter thirteen about a man named Ben who hit rock bottom, he had lost about everything. Ben has taken on a new attitude about life and God and maybe about us. He was a wheeler dealer but no time for God. First time I approached him about not working on Sundays and going to church he said he didn't believe in that stuff.

As time went on it got to the place where a mortgage company sold us Bens last 3000 acres. Bens son and grandson came to us for help to keep farming. They said unless we helped things were looking very bleak.

I was cautioned by bankers and friends that I could lose money, I figure if I can win this family over to Christianity it will be worth the risk. I have had good talks with Ben as we rode tractors and combines together. I asked Ben when he was going to start attending church. He promised me he is going with me when I get back from winter vacation. Ben has seen a difference in his son and grandchildren, he is thinking seriously.

MIRACLE 35 Early in the spring of 2007 Fern and I made a large pledge to donate to our local state family camp grounds. Getting closer to the time to pay I was wondering where to go for money. One ordinary day my secretary, June, walked into my office, asked me, did you pay that $40,000 note twice? No, I said. Well, said June, you deducted it twice from your check book. What a surprise, there was most of my pledge laying in my account. Let GOD have control of your check book.

MIRACLE 36 Fern and I have always been adventures and aggressive, 2007-08 was no different. One nice summer day in August 07, 2007 I asked Fern if she would go with me to Colorado to look at a farm. Yes, I don't want you to go alone, she said. We left Tuesday morning, got there Wednesday, looked at a farm. Bought one section, 640acres, and returned back home by Friday night. We had just signed a contract one hour before another buyer came around to buy. I had been talking to the realtor for several months for this property, the Lord held it several months for us.

You may wonder why I get so excited about farming. Farming to me is like hunting to a coon dog. Coon dogs are trained only to go after coon. They are not allowed to run after cars or cows or horses. They aren't allowed to play with children. They are kept locked up until a coon is in site. At that time, turned loose, they go through fences tearing their ears, they go over rock piles and through water ponds, they go through mud, thick brush, and thistles. They will do anything to get that last coon.

When I heard this story I was reminded of my farming. Farming has been my prime objective in life. Regardless of age or physical means, I would like to get just one more farm. I see the end as just one more big crop to harvest, and more money to give away. I feel my faith walk has been fortified by Genesis 8:22.

"While the earth remaineth
Seedtime and harvest
Cold and heat
Summer and winter
Day and night
Shall not cease."

Here it is 2009 and life and adventures are still going on. After reading the book , a friend of mine said to me, "the last chapter hasn't been written." He was right.

MIRACLE 37 Continuing the story of Ben mentioned on page 162. He was an entrepreneur that farmed thousands of acres, flew airplanes, including have his own personal Jet, and ran a commercial airplane crop spraying business. But had no time for God.

On page 220, Bens life of excessive material holdings had come to an end. Now he and his son were looking for financial help to try to keep farming, saying unless we helped , things looked very bleak and they would be out of business. They asked if we would cash rent the 5000 acres, some of which Ben owned at one time, that we had bought, and land that belonged to his brother, who owned the farm machinery and trucks, enough to farm the 5000 acres. To finance this size operation, both their half and our half, would take a million dollars a year.

We joined into a 50-50 share crop joint venture and have done this the past ten years. During these ten years, I began spending more time with Ben, riding together in tractors and combines. The only thing Ben had left for entertainment was driving equipment over the fields. Ben was temperamental. One day he would chew me out, he'd say in a mad tone, "you won't farm this land next year, I'll see to that," then maybe a week later he'd come back asking me to loan him money to buy a car or a house.

While riding around on tractors and combines, I asked Ben if he would go to church with me. He said, "I don't believe in that stuff." After several Sunday attempts, he did go to church with me. I picked him up in the morning and after church we had dinner together. Surprising enough, his son and grandchildren were there too.

In the fall of 2008 Ben began showing signs of health problems. At times he would look real yellow and we knew something was wrong. He started doctoring in December and was in and out of the hospital two times. In January he went in for the last time. I called and prayed with him. A few days later I called and questioned, "Ben it doesn't look good, does it?" He answered and said "No it doesn't look good." I asked him if he was going to Heaven. He didn't know. I prayed and he repeated after me a prayer of repentance and asked Jesus to forgive him. This was a great comfort to the surviving family as two days later he died. It appeared as though he was looking into a bright light as he peacefully passed on.

Thanking the Lord for this opportunity, I feel my mission, at least this one, has been completed. Having risked at least a million dollars, the Bible says one soul is worth more that the whole world.

MIRACLE 38 Another opportunity was made available to us in October, 2008, it was the elegant mansion at 1628 Elliot avenue in Minneapolis, which was built in 1887 as a home for the Benjamin Bull family. Mr. Bull was a respected businessman who was engaged in many businesses including farming and he introduced the first street railway in Minneapolis. The original cost of the 3-story brick and stone building and the 2-story wooden barn/carriage house was $27,000. It was recently appraised at $850,000. The building was placed in the ownership of North Central University by the generous donations of the Liechty family. Although we got it at a good discount, being investors, we did not have that kind of money lying around. The Lord prepared a miracle. Right after I made the first payment, from an unexpected source, I received more money than what the payment was. After I made the second payment, again from an unexpected source, I received a check equal to the amount of the payment. After I made the final payment, again from an unexpected source, I received an amount of money greater than my total cost of the project. I had no idea any of this money would be coming down the pike. We were surely blessed of the Lord. The mansion is currently housing the Intercultural Studies Department and the Business department which serves over 300 students in each of their majors.

As long as you keep active there are always some new experiences. In February 2009 we had 1000 acres of eight foot tall corn standing in the field. I went up to Minnesota where my crew was working. Combines were rolling in a foot of snow picking off the corn ears 30 inches above the ground. Temperatures were in the freezing mode, the snow did not stick to tires or other equipment. Trucks need to stay out on the roads, so the corn was hauled from combines to the trucks with a tractor and 1100 bu. grain cart. The corn was in good condition and drier than back in October, the normal harvest time.

MIRACLE 39 It was March 15, 2011 when my loving wife went to be with her Lord and Savior. She had battled with cancer for the last 2 ½ years. In memory of Fern, Sam Johnson and Jack Strom approached us about taking the major role in building a fitness center at Trinity Bible College in Ellendale, ND. When I heard the price, the thought hit me like a ton of bricks. I did not have a pile of money laying round that I could just throw in half a million dollars. I had stopped at Ellendale on my way to Oklahoma and maybe to Missouri to attend farm auctions. While driving and praying, Lord what should I do, in a little while I just got the gut feeling we could do it. I didn't hear any loud voice, just knew I should do it. I decided to do all three. Called Sam, and I made a promise to build the fitness center. I bought the farm in Oklahoma and later a farm in Missouri. The fitness center will carry Ferns name.

Trinity Bible College, Fern & Jon Liechty Fitness Center.

It amazes me how we can accept John 3:16 as a normal promise of Gods word and live our spiritual ups and downs and come back by faith in fellowship with our Lord. At the same time we stumble over Luke 6:38. Give and it shall be given unto you; good measure, pressed down, and shaken together, and running over, shall men give unto your bosom. For with the same measure that ye mete withal it shall be measured to you again.

Proverbs 3:5-6 Trust in the Lord with all thy heart and lean not unto thy own understanding. In all thy ways acknowledge Him, and he shall direct thy paths.

A man was leaning against a high pole, his ear tight against the pole, standing there as if he was hearing something. After a few hours I thought I better check this out. Let me try it as I put my ear against the pole. I listened ever putting my ear tighter to the pole I said I can't hear anything. Oh, he said, It has been that way all day. YOU MUST LEAN ON JESUS.

A man going into business promised his Pastor and God, if he was blessed, would give 10% of the profits to the church. First year he made $1000 gave $100 to church. Second year made $10,000 gave $1000 to church. Third year made $100,000 gave $10,000 to church. Fourth year made $1,000,000 gave $100,000 to church. Fifth year made $5,000,000, went to the pastor and asked him to pray to God to undo his promise, he said he just couldn't give $500,000 away. The pastor knelt down in front of him and prayed silently, when he got up the man asked him if he prayed to get him relief, no said the pastor, I asked God to reduce your income to a level where you can give 10%

MIRACLE 40 James Valley Youth For Christ in Jamestown, ND was in need of more room for their activities for the youth attending the center. There was room on the back side of their property to build a one/half basket ball court center. Along with the center they added handicap access and new rest rooms to the center. This project was completed and dedicated in September, 2013. The Liechty family had the honor and privilege of supplying most of the funds for the addition. Rather than having a ribbon cutting ceremony, I was honored to throw the first basket ball through the basket ball hoop that was covered with a ribbon. This is a much needed beautiful addition.

MIRACLE 41 Several months after Fern passed away I was at ND Camp Meeting. With my newly purchased convertible truck I was offering rides for 99 cents to raise money for a camp program. Among riders was Elsie Wurgler from Minot, ND who put in a whole three dollars. We having a business in Minot, ND I asked her if we could have lunch sometime and she agreed. This was the beginning of a courtship that ended in marriage on November,24th 2012 December 18th we left Minot on our Honeymoon heading for Florida. Driving through Nebraska we stopped for lunch with our farmers there. After lunch we headed south on Hwy 183 running into a snow storm near Ansley, NE looking for motel to park for the night, road signs all frozen over with snow and ice that we couldn't read, at speeds of 45 to 50 came to dead end in the road. Applied the brakes on solid ice, went straight off the eight foot dead end cliff. Sailing 40 feet through the air we landed in a corn field on all four wheels going through an electric fence.

The Chrysler van still in motion I stepped on accelerator and kept driving through the corn field back out through the electric fence, through a road ditch, and back up on the road. On the road we stopped to evaluate what really happened. The right front door wouldn't close, Elsie held it shut till we got to a body shop at Broken Bow NE, where we spent the night. The right back door would not open and hood was sprung sideways and would not open. We drove all the way to Florida in that condition. When repairing the van they found a bent rear axle, cracked radiator, front bumper gone, left rear quarter panel missing and many body paint scratches needing to repaint ¾ of the body.

We are thankful we didn't have serious bodily injury, we feel there were many Angels watching over us.

MIRACLE 42 The opportunities for giving were still coming along. In November, 2012 Pebbles Thompson asked me to go to lunch with her and Darin. Knowing somewhat of the ministry she was doing with abused children I felt there would be money involved. I turned down the lunch opportunity and soon after left for Florida. After a month in Florida, Elsie and I went to Texas till the end of March, then back to North Dakota. All this time passed and I couldn't shake the thought of turning down Pebbles. Again in May Pebbles asked to see me and I turned her down again. Now I felt I was arguing with the Lord about money. Again I couldn't shake the idea so in June I called Pebbles and wanted to talk, She

School building purchased for Pebble Thompson's ministry.

had a vacated school property she was trying to buy, by this time she had negotiated a price well under half a million. I think my stalling may have saved us all some money. The Lord put a figure in my mind so I wrote the check.

MIRACLE 43 Thirty days after I wrote the check a man we had never talked to or heard of made us an offer on some real estate, which we had never thought of selling, offering twenty times as much as we had paid for the property which came into mega, mega, dollars. You can't out give the Lord.

Jon and Elsie Liechty on their wedding day in 2012

/FOURTEEN/
EVER GREATFUL

In conclusion, I would like to give a general statement. I thank the Lord that he could use a poor farm boy, who was chided a few times, with only a 9th-grade education. I believe my success began the time I made an altar before the Lord on the ocean liner, crossing the Atlantic ocean, at sea level, asking Him to come into my heart and guide my life, YOU TOO CAN DO THIS TOO. I believe we need to take the Bible literally. Jesus wasn't joking when He said He would give us the desires of our heart or that it is more blessed to give than to receive and to love your neighbor as yourself. Then too, the walk and talk I had with Jesus where I promised to faithfully give according to the way He would bless me.

In the beginning, more than 50 years ago, we started giving 20 percent of our profits away to charities. We were able to increase that both percentage-wise and dollar-wise as the years passed by. The last few years we have given up to 50 percent. We are currently supporting over 50 missionaries, churches and charities on a monthly basis and write checks each month for the same. Elsie and my own goals are to continue this pattern for as long as we both have good health.

"It's not what you'd do with the million
If fortune should ere be your lot,
But what you are doing with the
Dollar and quarter you've got."

-Mickey Carter

Our blessings have been phenomenal. Our giving to missions has opened up avenues of travel into over 40 countries on five continents. We have been on boats, cruise ships, submarines, airplanes—commercial and private, large and small.

"Money is like love; you must give it away, to get it."

-Jon Liechty

I LOVE TO LIVE
Today, dear Lord, I'm 80
And there's much I haven't done.
I hope dear Lord, you'll let me live until I'm 81
But then, if I haven't finished all I want to do.
Would You please let me stay a while, until I'm
Eighty two.
So many places I want to go, so very much to see,
Do You think You could manage to make it 83?
The world is changing very fast,
there is so much in store,
I'd like it very much to live until I'm 84.
And if by then I'm still alive, I'd like to stay 'til
Eighty five.
More planes will be up in the air,
So I'd really like to stick
And see what happens to the world when I turn
Eighty six.
I know, dear Lord, it's much to ask,
(and it must be nice in Heaven)
Please let me stay to eighty seven.
I know by then I won't be fast,
And sometimes will be late,
But it would be so pleasant to be around at 88.

I will have seen so many things,
And I've had a wonderful time.
So, I'm sure that I'll be willing to leave
At the age of 89…Maybe.
Just one more thing I'd like to say,
dear Lord I thank you kindly.
But if it's okay with You, I'd love to live past 90.
I now am just three month short of being there.

Looking back over the past 90 years, I am a blest man to have completed this book. My health is strong, blood pressure is normal, I don't think I am afflicted with Alzheimer's, but I do have a few some-timers. We have been blessed with several farming and business goals. One of my goals which started in my early custom combine days was I always thought it good to own a farm in each state from Texas to North Dakota. That would be six states. The farms didn't line up quite in that order, but the Lord gave us farms in twelve states including Montana. It might be interesting to note that in our early days of farming, a man said one-time that if I didn't like to fix equipment, I shouldn't be a farmer. Considering that, things went pretty well on the farm. The Lord always gave me hired help that could fix. I didn't need to. It goes back to proper connections. Jesus has allowed me to drive machines, mostly pickup trucks, through the fields and enjoy His great creation.

Some people judge your success by the size of your house or the kind of toys you own. How big a home could we build if we put all of our money into a house each year, rather than giving the money to charities? I like to think I'm building my mansion in Heaven. If I don't get a mansion there, it will be worth it all to see JESUS. A friend of mine asked me if I thought he would go to Heaven. I replied, it depends on what YOU do with Jesus. Everyone wants to go to Heaven, but many shy away from Jesus, I don't think it works that way.

You might say acquiring property is no miracle, and maybe not. Although the greatest miracle is the fact that we have been able to give away millions of dollars to charity while expanding our business. You won't see a miracle if you don't look for one.

"In everything you do, put God first
and He will direct you
and crown your efforts with success"
(Proverbs 3:6)

I would like to challenge you to try to give 20% of your profits to all kinds of charities, be sure they are trust worthy and believe like you do that God blesses a faithful giver, and keep good records of your giving. Try it and see if 80% won't go farther than the 100%. It's not enough to throw in a 10 or 20 dollar bill or write an occasional check for your offering. Treat your giving like you treat your utility bills. If you borrow money to pay your running expenses, borrow enough to pay your tithes and offerings too. That is your test of faith. Keep an accurate record. If you don't give 10 percent you are robbing God, (Malachi 3:8), as you start exceeding the 10 percent, that's when the Lord will look at you with favor. You must seek and pray for divine guidance as you give, so that your funds are directed to the right place. I have NOT written this book to exalt myself. Without the help of the Lord, my wife, our children, my brothers, many friends and neighbors, all of the above would not have happened. I still feel inadequate for most of this story.

The Lord is good, a strong hold
In the day of trouble; and he
knows them that trust in him.

Nahum 1:7

There are some of you guys and gals that haven't made a full commitment to Jesus Christ, you are somewhere between faith and failure, you are on a rough road, get off the fence. I urge you, make an altar, ask Jesus to forgive your sins and let Him come into your heart and life. Your church, your pastor, or your good works alone won't get you into Heaven. You need to settle it with Jesus yourself. You can talk to Jesus like any other person. He is waiting for you, it really is the best life.

THE END

Jon and his toys at age 80.

/MORE MEMORIES/

Moose and Dall sheep from Alaska. Elk from Montana.

Main farm service truck, Arthur used for service in South Dakota.

Picture of Mom and Dad shortly before Dad got sick with cancer.

Fern by our church on 8th Ave and 8th St, Jamestown

TO ORDER THIS BOOK CALL
701 320 3081
OR WRITE
JON LIECHTY
PO Box 690
JAMESTOWN, ND 58402
Or use BARNES AND NOBLE WEBSITE
www.bn.com